P9-DDZ-864

Hive Management History Series: No. 42

INDUSTRIAL LEADERSHIP

BY

H. L. GANTT

ADDRESSES DELIVERED IN THE PAGE LECTURE SERIES, 1915, BEFORE THE SENIOR CLASS OF THE SHEFFIELD SCIENTIFIC SCHOOL, YALE UNIVERSITY

EASTON
HIVE PUBLISHING COMPANY
1974

Library of Congress Cataloging in Publication Data

Gantt, Henry Laurence, 1861-1919.
Industrial leadership.

(Hive management history series, no. 42)
Reprint of the 1921 ed. published by Association Press, New York, in series: Page lecture series, 1915.
1. Industrial management — Addresses, essays, lectures. I. Title. II. Series: Page lecture series, 1915.
HD31.G27 1973 658.4 72-9507
ISBN 0-87960-044-6

Manufactured in the United States of America

TO THE MEMORY OF

COL. WILLIAM ALLAN

THE "DOCTOR ARNOLD" OF AMERICA

CONTENTS

LIST OF ILLUSTRATIONS

FOREWORD

The great war now being waged in Europe is making clear the superiority which autocracy has had in the past in its ability to organize a nation for both industrial and military efficiency.

If democracy is to compete successfully with autocracy in the long run, it must develop organizing and executive methods which will be at least equal to those of autocracy.

In this course of lectures I have tried to set forth the principles on which I believe an industrial democracy can be based which will be even more effective than any system of industrialism which can be developed under autocracy.

One of the most important questions which I have raised is, how far the state should go with industrial and vocational training. It is generally conceded that it is the function of the state to give such broad general training as is applicable to our industries in general, but that it is a function of the industries themselves to give as much of the training which is special to those industries as it is possible for them to give, and to rely upon the state only for that residuum which cannot be given by the industries themselves.

Before the state commits itself to schemes for vocational training, it is exceedingly important that an effort be made to make this residuum as small as possible, and it is surprising how much more can be done in industries by the methods herein outlined than has generally been thought possible, and how good are the results.

H. L. Gantt.

December 11, 1915.

INDUSTRIAL LEADERSHIP

I

INDUSTRIAL LEADERSHIP

I have chosen the subject of Industrial Leadership as my first lecture because I wish to emphasize it over all other elements that make for industrial progress. What statesman, or warrior, ever produced such permanently far-reaching results in the world as any one of the great industrial leaders so well known to us—Watt, Fulton, Whitney, Stephenson, Morse, Bessemer, Siemens, Bell, Edison, Westinghouse, Wright? These great inventors were pioneers, but the host that developed their inventions to the high state of perfection which they have attained are not less valuable members of society. Indeed, we have today so much undigested and unutilized knowledge that I am inclined to think that the man who shows us how to use it satisfactorily is quite as important as he who discovers it.

It is these great men and their followers that during the past forty years have absolutely revolutionized the conditions of life. Forty years ago the great majority of our people lived on farms, and were, to a large extent, themselves producing the necessities of life; today they are collected into large communities and engaged in special occupations which do not directly supply their needs. In fact the great mass of people buy almost everything they use. This result has come to pass because we have changed from an agricultural community, largely to a manufacturing, or industrial community.

This progressive change, which is still rapidly going on, has introduced problems for the solution of which there is no precedent. Modern industrialism is so modern that its greatest problems have hardly been clearly grasped even by those who have given them most study.

Twenty years ago the financier thought he had found a panacea for most of the evils which the new developments began to show, in his combination of industrial plants into large organizations. Undoubtedly he did succeed for a while in securing a larger profit for the promoters of the organizations; but the most important problems, those concerning the relations of employer to employee, have not been solved any better by the large corporation than by the individual employer. In fact the large corporation seems in many cases to have accentuated the troubles which had arisen. This has undoubtedly been due, in a large measure, to the lack of personal touch between employer and employee, which seems impossible in the large corporations, where there was at first an apparent tendency to ignore entirely the human factor as an influence in industrial work.

Men who promoted these large corporations were in many cases financiers or merchants, who previously had dealt almost exclusively with money and goods. They had bought in the cheapest markets and sold at the best price they could get. Their natural tendency, therefore, was to apply to the purchase of labor the same rules which they had applied to the purchase of materials, namely, to buy it as cheaply as possible. The great difficulty which stood in the way of accomplishing this result was that there was no exact means of measuring the labor received, and the best that could be done was to buy a man's time, on the theory that time consumed was a measure of labor performed. While this is in a measure correct if the workman feels that he is being equitably rewarded for the work done, it may be far from correct when he does not have this feeling. When he realizes, as is often the case, that the employer, taking advantage of his necessity, gives him the smallest hourly rate he can be hired for, he naturally does only just enough work to hold his job.

Moreover, there has seldom been any attempt to keep a record of the work any man did in order that a more equitable compensation might be accorded him; and, whether he did much or little, he was accorded the hourly rate of wages common to his class. The railroad companies, perhaps more than any other organizations, have offended in this manner, and the rates of wages, which they were willing to pay for different classes of workmen were not only fixed by employers, but maintained with all their power. A mechanic, therefore, had but little chance of getting a higher compensation than his class rate, no matter how industrious or conscientious he might be.

The introduction of piece work, by which the workman was paid for the work he did, instead of the time he worked, promised better results; but, as piece prices were commonly set on a basis of what had been done by a man dissatisfied with his daily wage, it soon became clear that the men could do much more work than had been done, and earned correspondingly higher wages, with the result that *the employer reduced the price per piece.* This "cutting" of piece prices was common practice whenever the workman earned much more than his class rate; and the capable workman, recognizing the impossibility of increasing his compensation through more, or better work, soon ceased to make any effort in that direction, and devoted his spare time to the organization of a union with the object of advancing the class rate.

A careful consideration of this subject will show that the employers who insisted on class rates, irrespective of the ability and service of the individuals themselves, thus furnished the strongest incentive for the formation of the unions, which have been, and are now, so effective in increasing the class rate, and which have done much for the amelioration of the condition of the workmen.

The neglect on the part of the employer to recognize individual ability, and to reward it correspondingly, coupled with his effort to secure workmen at the lowest possible daily wage rate, forced the workman to concentrate his attention on the wages he received, and made him comparatively indifferent to the amount of work he did. In other words, both employer and employee ignored to a large extent the amount of work done, and devoted their efforts, the one to paying as little wages as possible, and the other to getting as much as possible for the work he did.

Under such conditions it is not surprising that costs should be high, and that there should be antagonism between employer and employee. It is, of course, impossible to pay permanently high wages unless a large amount of work is done for those wages. At first the workmen apparently did not see this, nor did the employer see that there was no advantage to him in forcing workmen to work at low wages, for by so doing, he failed to get a proper return even for the small wage he paid. *Both employer and employee thus put a premium on inefficiency.*

Within the past ten years this portion of the subject has been given much more attention, and it is becoming recognized among the most progressive manufacturers of the day, that the ratio between the wages paid and the work done is more important than the absolute amount of wages paid, and that the absolute amount of work done is more important than either.

Moreover, it is becoming recognized that the good man at high wages not only does more work per dollar of wages than the poor man at low wages, but better work. In the most prosperous factories, and those turning out the highest grade of product, we invariably find high-grade, well-paid workmen; while in those factories which are making but little profit, and where the work is of a poor quality, the workmen are usually poorly paid and of low grade. The unsuccessful manufacturer, when this matter is pointed out to him, too often says that the successful owner can afford to hire good men at high wages, because he is successful. Evidence seems to indicate, however, that he is successful because he hires the good men at high wages, and that the policy of paying satisfactory wages has been more influential in producing low costs than any other item.

This leads us to the broad subject of administration, and we naturally ask if there are any general principles on which successful business administration is based. This subject has been much discussed, but the factors ordinarily entering into the success of an industrial enterprise are so varied that it is often hard to say which has been the most important one in producing the success obtained.

If there is any one principle, which more than any other, is influential in promoting the success of an organization it is the following:

The authority to issue an order involves the responsibility to see that it is properly executed.

The system of management which we advocate is based on this principle, which eliminates "bluff" as a feature in management, for a man can only assume the responsibility for doing a thing properly when he not only knows how to do it, but can also teach somebody else to do it.

The fact that our system of management sooner or later exposes the bluffer makes its installation in a factory very difficult, for there is in every organization, especially when it is large, a surprisingly large proportion of bluffers, who are smart enough to see promptly that under such a principle they will not last very long. Moreover, the higher up they are, the quicker they are affected.

Professor E. D. Jones of the University of Michigan has recently written a series of articles which are now published in a book entitled "The Business Administrator," in which he attempts to segregate the principles of administration. While his success has apparently not been entirely complete in this matter, yet he has made clear some very important facts, the first of which is, that administration means administration of human affairs, and that the one common element in all enterprises is the human element. The materials and forces with which we deal are comparatively unimportant, being subject to laws which in general have been pretty definitely determined. Our knowledge, however, of the best methods of handling men is still far from complete. In order to collect data on this subject, Professor Jones has studied the great leaders and administrators of the past of whom history gives us an account. He has developed the fact, that in the past, great success of co-operative human effort has been attained only under great leaders. Even a casual study of industrialism today indicates that leadership performs a most important function.

A few years ago there was a strong feeling in this country that the most important element in any enterprise was the financial element, and that if there was only money enough available, nothing else mattered very much. This idea has not held good, for we are beginning to realize that there is an end to the largest bank account, and are rapidly coming to the conclusion that neither money nor organization will permanently insure success without proper direction. It is therefore imperative upon us to study leadership, and to find the laws on which successful administration is based.

The absolute necessity for proper leadership in industry thus becomes clear, and we begin to see a close parallel to leadership in war, the necessity for which today is becoming increasingly apparent. History has given us very accurate accounts of great generals, and it is of this class of leadership that we can learn most. After a little study we realize that leadership in war and leadership in industry are not only based on the same principles, but are equally important. It seems therefore that in order to give this subject the attention it deserves, we should profit by the account that history gives us of great warriors. Industrial leadership has been largely overlooked in the past for the reason that accidental conditions have in many cases been quite as effective in securing wealth as leadership. Such opportunities are, however, no longer numerous, especially in our industries, and a study of industrial leadership is forcing itself upon us.

Just as war is the great training school for those who are to make war, so industry is the great training school for those who are to create industry. Leaders in war and in industry hold the same relative importance in their respective spheres. If this is the case, it is well for us to see what the greatest warrior of modern times has to say about the importance of leadership in war, and thus arrive at some appreciation of the importance of leadership in industry. Napoleon said:

> In war men are nothing; it is the man who is everything. The general is the head, the whole of any army. It was not the Roman army that conquered Gaul, but Cæsar; it was not the Carthaginian army that made Rome tremble in her gates, but Hannibal; it was not the Macedonian army that

reached the Indus, but Alexander; it was not the French army that carried the war to the Weser and the Inn, but Turenne; it was not the Prussian army which, for seven years, defended Prussia against the three greatest Powers of Europe, but Frederick the Great.

The historian in making this quotation stated that Napoleon reiterated a truth confirmed by the experience of successive ages, *that a wise direction is of more avail than overwhelming numbers, sound strategy than the most perfect armament.* Similarly in industry—*a wise policy is of more avail than a large plant; good management, than perfect equipment.*

The historian goes on to say:

Even a professional army of long standing and old traditions is what its commander makes it; its character sooner or later becomes the reflex of his own; from him the officers take their tone; his energy or his inactivity, his firmness or vacillation, are rapidly communicated even to the lower ranks; and so far-reaching is the influence of the leader, that those who record his campaigns concern themselves but little, as a rule, with the men who followed him. The history of famous armies is the history of great generals, for no army has ever achieved great things unless it has been well commanded. If the general be second-rate, the army also will be second-rate.

These facts in military history have their exact counterpart in industrialism, for THE FACTORY INVARIABLY REFLECTS THE MANAGER. The real problem of today is, then, how to select and train, or rather how to train and select our industrial leaders.

Professor Jones states the indisputable fact that *the possession of wealth and hence power, does not necessarily fit a man for leadership.* There is a general feeling, however, that because our industries have in the past been directed in an autocratic manner, that autocracy will continue to be the rule, and that there is apparently no escape from it. This feeling seems to be quite widespread, and to be substantiated by the marvelous industrial development of Germany under autocratic rule. While it is possible that autocracy in industry is the final stage, I do not think the case is by any means proven. Has not the development of industrial organization been in a large measure parallel to the development of political organization? In both, we had individualism; then paternalism; and then tribalism, or something approximating it; next we had autocracy. In our political organization we have passed one step beyond—we, in this country, believe in democracy, and the great struggle now going on in Europe is largely a question as to whether democracy or autocracy shall be the final phase in the old world.

The marvelous efficiency of Germany as an industrial and military nation has claimed the attention of the whole world; but we must realize that Germany is the only nation which has made any serious attempt at national organization of industry. When, therefore, we compare the industrial condition of Germany with the industrial conditions of any other country, we are not comparing one organization with another, but a highly perfected organization with lack of organization.

In the summer of 1913, three hundred members of the American Society of Mechanical Engineers visited Germany at the invitation of the "*Verein deutscher Ingenieure.*" We spent three weeks touring the country and visited most of their great cities, where we were entertained with the greatest possible hospitality, and had thrown open to us many of their most successful industrial plants.

We were much impressed with what we saw, and the universal prevalence of system and order elicited our unbounded admiration.

When, however, we came to the consideration of the industrial plants as units, we were in almost entire accord that, with the exception of a few industries, plant for plant, America had nothing to fear from Germany.

The greatest power in Germany in the past has been that of their autocratic rulers, who not only encouraged scientific development, but demanded it, and used all the power of the state to further it. This tendency rapidly brought Germany to the front in the scientific world, and the application of the scientific knowledge thus attained has brought her to the front in both the industrial and the military world. How effective autocratic power may become in the industrial world when guided by science we have long known, but it is only recently that we have realized how effective such a power might become in a military world under the same guidance.

The goal for which Germany is now striving by military power seemed to many of us much more likely of attainment through their industrial development, for the rapidity with which industrial development can be carried on by autocratic means is far greater than that which has so far been possible under democratic methods. On the other hand, the results obtained under democratic methods are far more permanent and less liable to be perverted to false ends.

This leads us, therefore, to ask if autocracy in industry is not just as much a phase in industrial development, as we in this country consider it to be in political development.

As a matter of fact, during the past ten years it has been my effort to introduce methods of equal opportunity into industry, and to select leaders in the most democratic manner possible. I am pleased to say that the efficiency of the organization thus produced has seemed to be almost in direct proportion to the success of introducing the method of equal opportunity for selecting leaders.

Too little work has been done in this line, and there are too few results available to allow us to make any very strong statements, but the success so far attained is such as to make us feel that we are on the right track, and that the nation, which first does away with autocracy and special privilege, will take the lead in industrialism.

The scientific method thrives best when all have equal opportunity, and our chance of getting proper industrial leaders is far greater when we have a whole people to choose from than if they are to be selected from any one class.

Professor Jones' emphasis of the fact that in all problems of administration the most important element is the human element, compels acceptance of the democratic idea, for no manager can attain the highest ideals unless he is thoroughly familiar with all the elements with which he has to deal. It is general experience that unless men are studied from a democratic standpoint, the student fails to get a proper appreciation of the human element.

This brings me to what I consider one of the most important activities of the Sheffield Scientific School, namely, the Social Service Work which was described in Professor Roe's paper before the American Society of Mechanical Engineers at their meeting in St. Paul in June, 1914.

I like the title "Social Service Work."

All of the engineer's work is *service work*—in that he makes his living by serving somebody, and much is *social service work,* for in much of what he does, he serves the community. This is not exactly the meaning of the title of Professor Roe's paper, but it gives me an opportunity to emphasize the fact that in an organized community we all earn our living by giving service. When one man hires another it is his service he wants. When a man buys a machine it is the service of that machine he wants—not the specific machine—any other machine which could perform the same service equally well and equally economically would do.

In a civilized country we are all buying and selling service. The bread we eat, and the coal we burn are available to us through the service of many people. Likewise our value to the community is measured by the service we render, and in the long run our reward is apt to be in proportion to that service.

"Social Service Work," although narrower in meaning than what I have described, is not only a most excellent method of bringing together the workman and the future leader, but of producing in the mind of the student a conception of the pleasure and value of serving. This is a comparatively new idea to many people, and its growth is fostered only under democratic conditions. Under autocratic methods to render service is a sign of inferiority; the man of power compels the service of others. Under democratic methods the man of power uses that power to serve others. Under autocratic rule the man in authority is a master; under democratic rule he is a servant.

Engineering schools have successfully taught the laws of materials and forces, and the methods of adapting these materials and forces to the use of man; but they have almost entirely disregarded the human element, a knowledge of which is absolutely essential for the proper utilization of any mechanisms which the engineer may contrive. If we would direct successfully the operation of any mechanism, we must have as complete knowledge of the men who are going to operate it as we have of the mechanism itself, and the Social Service Work, which has become such a feature in this Institution, is, to my mind, the best available method of supplementing the knowledge obtained in the classroom.

Without an intimate knowledge of the workman, a college graduate is too apt to assume, because the workman has not the same kind of knowledge that he has, that he is necessarily ignorant and a fit subject for contempt. A little association with him, however, soon dispels this idea, for the college man finds out that although the workman's knowledge may be quite different from the knowledge that he has, it is very extensive, and embraces subjects of which he is entirely ignorant. The workman has indeed a great deal of knowledge, much of which is far more practical and better suited to his needs than that the college man can give him. Moreover, the workman readily recognizes that the college man knows but little about those subjects with which he is most familiar, and the contempt which the college man is apt to get for the workman before he knows him is only a small fraction of the contempt which the workman frequently gets for the college man.

The Social Service Work which has attracted the interest of so many of our men is certainly the best way which has yet been devised to enable the college man and the workman to learn to know and to appreciate the good qualities of each other. The college man is too apt to feel that by reading a few books on industrialism, or political economy, that he has acquired a broad knowledge of working conditions, but he very soon finds that many of the general principles so widely exploited in such books, produce, in special cases, results which are not even hinted at in the books.

The fact that the average wage rate in an industry is high, does not at all prove that there may not be quite as much, or more, suffering in that industry than in an industry in which the average wage rate is much lower.

I have confidence that some of the men trained in industrial service work will thereby be enabled to see more clearly the proper relations between employer and employee, and in the near future will contribute much to the solution of our industrial problems.

In the past much emphasis has been laid upon the importance of our "captains of industry," and other men who have attained great wealth through industrial enterprises. A few years ago their methods were extensively advertised in the magazines, and they were as a class pretty generally looked up to.

Times have changed, however, and the world has advanced. Mr. Rockefeller's method of acquiring his fortune was not greatly different from the methods pursued by other men in his day. He was only just a little more shrewd, and perhaps a little more ruthless. The same thing may be said of Mr. Harriman and Mr. Carnegie, but I believe the time is past when the methods of these three prominent figures can ever be duplicated. The industrial leader of the future must practice methods which are approved by the people, and they must be such as not to take unfair advantage of anybody. The term "unfair competition" has gained much publicity of late. It is similar to spiking a man in a game of baseball.

As was said before, the world advances through leadership, and I feel that it is just as much the function of our engineering schools to train our industrial leaders as it is that of our military schools to train our military leaders.

This being the case, our engineering schools should have a broad knowledge of all matters affecting our industrial system.

Until recently our financiers, on account of the power of their wealth, have exercised almost complete control of our industrial institutions, and have too often dominated not only the financial and selling policies, but the policy employed in handling workmen. Of the first two subjects they frequently had quite a good deal of knowledge, but it is seldom that their knowledge of industrial conditions was such as to enable them to formulate an intelligent policy where the workmen are concerned. This fact is coming to be more and more recognized, and the handling of the workmen is being delegated more and more to those who have made a study of the subject.

The fact, as stated before, that our industries have been handled in general in an autocratic manner is no sign that they will continue to be so handled, and almost every day we see increasing symptoms that people are realizing what true democracy means.

None of us today really believe that men are created equal, but we do believe that they are entitled to an equal opportunity. Moreover, developments seem to indicate that the more nearly we can accord men equal opportunities for advancement, the more prosperous the individuals and the country as a whole will be.

This seems to make incumbent upon the engineering schools a thorough study of all industrial conditions. Books on political economy are all very well, but in most cases they were written before the advent of modern industrialism, or by people who have too many times studied it from the academic standpoint. Every opportunity, therefore, should be given to the student to study the conditions at first hand as they exist today in our industries, for by such a course only can the industrial leader of the future acquire such knowledge as will enable him to inspire confidence in those whom he will be called upon to lead.

As I look back over my own history I can pick out five or six men who have influenced my life more than all others combined; some of these were school teachers, some college professors and others were in industry. Each man in this audience may have, probably will have, marked influence on the lives of a large number of workmen. People learn but little from what they are told, but they readily imitate what appeals to them. If, therefore, a man would be a leader he must know thoroughly the people whom he would lead, and be able to shape his actions in such a manner that they will not only be understood but thoroughly appreciated by his followers.

In a paper on "Training Workmen in Habits of Industry and Cooperation" read before the American Society of Mechanical Engineers in December, 1908, I made the following statement: "The general policy of the past has been to drive, but the era of force must give way to that of knowledge, and the policy of the future will be to teach and to lead, to the advantage of all concerned." I did not then realize how rapidly my prediction would come true.

As an illustration of the difference between leading and driving, I may cite an incident that occurred in my presence in a steel foundry. For the benefit of those who may not know, I may say that steel is poured through a nozzle in the bottom of a ladle, and not over the top as is the case of cast iron. This nozzle is closed with a plug, but for one reason or another this plug sometimes does not close the nozzle entirely after pouring a mold, and the steel leaking out splashes over the ground and the flasks, not only making the neighborhood of the ladle a very hot place, but setting fire to anything combustible within reach.

In order to protect himself from being burnt, should a "bad shut off" occur, the ladleman usually wears thick woolen clothes, including, if possible, an old overcoat.

On the occasion in mind the "shut off," while the ladle was being taken from one mold to the next, was very bad, and the splashing and the heat of the molten steel were almost unbearable.

It must be understood that a leaky nozzle is very apt to "freeze" up, not only leaving the molds unpoured, but leaving the steel in the ladle in a large solid mass which it is very difficult to utilize. Moreover, the flasks to be poured are usually needed by the molders the next day, so if they are not poured it is usually impossible to get a full day's work molded the following day.

Notwithstanding these facts, which the ladleman knew perfectly well, he decided that he could not face the heat of the steel from the leaky nozzle, and left his ladle hanging on the crane with the steel running out.

The superintendent, who was standing near, did not say anything; but, signaling to the craneman to move to the next mold, went up, and taking the handle of the ladle began to pour the metal. Before he had finished pouring the first mold, the ladleman came up, and taking the handle poured the remainder of the heat.

The flying sparks had ruined a suit of clothes, but the superintendent had established himself in the estimation of the workmen, and the ladleman as far as I know never again forsook his post.

This is a good example of physical leadership, which, while absolutely essential to any kind of success, can only affect the few people who are immediately concerned. There is another and higher leadership, that of the intellect, by which the methods and thoughts of one man may affect the whole civilized world. Industrial leaders who have most prominently attracted our attention in the past are those who have, by their inventions or their direction of activities, accumulated large fortunes; but none of these are as great as the man who by the force of his intellect leads people throughout the civilized world to benefit themselves and others. Such a man was the late Frederick Winslow Taylor who, in his determination to eliminate error and to base our industrial relations on fact, set an example which will have an effect all over the world.

His great contribution to the world's work was to substitute knowledge of human activities for opinion as a basis of action.

His insistence that all industrial questions could be best answered by a scientific investigation was at first scoffed at by many of our industrial leaders, and it was nearly twenty years before he got much support. Now, however, at the end of thirty-five years his persistence is bearing fruit so rapidly that the whole industrial world is undergoing a revolution due to his ideas.

His death cut short the activities of a man who had the welfare of his fellow man at heart, and who spent much of his life in trying to establish a basis on which the relations between employer and employee could be made mutually satisfactory.

When he began his work, almost all such relations were established by opinions. Today there are few industries in which fact has not supplanted many opinions.

He had the feeling that waste was a crime, and that efficiency in work was a duty not only to ourselves and to our employers, but to the community at large.

His name will live as that of a man who could rise above individual cases, and grasp general laws that would make for the happiness and prosperity of all.

We cannot all be Taylors, but each of us can add his little mite to the sum of industrial knowledge with the confident expectation that it will ultimately be used for the benefit of mankind. I earnestly recommend the reading of Mr. Taylor's writings as a preparation for your life work.

TRAINING WORKMEN

II

TRAINING WORKMEN

In my last lecture I emphasized the importance of leadership, and the responsibility of engineering schools for the training of industrial leaders. Many men, however, who rise to leadership in industry have not had the benefit of a technical education, and consequently lack the special training to be had only in technical schools. For a long time to come, and perhaps always, a large number of industrial leaders will be men who have had only an elementary school education. It is therefore necessary in the adoption of methods for the training of workmen to bear in mind that many men have the natural ability to become leaders if only they have set before them the proper ideals, methods, and opportunity.

Napoleon claimed that one of the principal elements of the success of his armies was the fact that every common soldier carried the baton of a marshal in his haversack.

In the same way the success of our industries, and hence of the country, will in a large measure depend upon the opportunity for the man in the ranks to better himself, and the methods of training so far as the state contributes to them should be such as to enable him to take advantage of that opportunity. How far it is the duty of the state to compel individual employers or corporations, to conform to this standard may be open to debate, but I feel that in the long run they will get the greatest benefit by conforming to it absolutely.

The widespread adoption of the public school system has committed our country to the responsibility of training our youth intellectually, and the time seems rapidly approaching when the state will assume the responsibility for training the youth in manual dexterity. There is no question that this is the logical outcome of our industrial conditions, and one of the problems which faces us, is just how far the state should go in special training. In other words, if the state accepts the responsibility for industrial training, how far shall it accept the responsibility for vocational training?

Just as some knowledge of engineering and

of industrial processes has become one of the essentials of a liberal education, so also is an elementary knowledge of the use of the ordinary tools of our common industries becoming an essential part of any education.

It is my feeling, however, that when our public school system has given this general training, it has assumed all the responsibility for the training of workmen that can be legitimately put upon it. Any additional training must have special reference to a particular industry, and is generally termed vocational training. Such training it is the function of the industries themselves to give; but in order that a workman may develop himself to the best advantage, vocational training should always be preceded by industrial training, which gives him the ability to learn more than one trade with surprising rapidity, and thus develops in him a spirit of independence and self-reliance, the value of which it is hard to overestimate.

The rapidly changing conditions in our industries, which make it necessary that the workman shall be able to adapt himself readily to new conditions, emphasize the importance of the more general industrial training as a precedent to vocational training, which without the former is apt to make many men slaves of the industry in which they were trained. Such men suffer a great hardship when a change of industrial conditions throws out of employment those whose limited training makes them unfitted for any other industry.

Aside from this viewpoint, it is the duty of the state as a whole to see that our training methods are such as will make the most valuable citizens. In order to determine what course the state should take to accomplish this result, we must ask what qualities in the workman are most beneficial to the state as a whole.

In order to answer that question, I will tell of a story I heard years ago of a well-known Baltimore judge who went to visit a friend in one of the southern counties of Maryland, a large part of which is composed of sand hills and pines. His host met him at the steamboat wharf, and as they were driving slowly homeward through the deep sand of the road, the judge finally said, "What do you raise in this country, anyhow?" He got the reply:

"Raise men."

This answer showed a deep insight in the

most important problem of all ages. *That country which, as a whole, has the best men will surely assert its supremacy in the long run.* As far as the state is concerned, therefore, in its connection with industries, it should carry out that policy which has the tendency to produce the highest grade of men.

Wealth is convenient, luxury is pleasant; but the nation which does not so develop its industries as to produce men, will not for any great length of time hold its place in the world. The Roman Empire, just before its fall, had wealth and luxury in abundance; but wealth and luxury both have enervating tendencies, and the empire succumbed before the strong manhood of the Goths.

It is imperative, therefore, in seeking the proper industrial methods to bear in mind the fact that the *men produced by them are far more important to the life and prosperity of a nation than the wealth and luxury by which we set so much store.* We, as a nation, have been accused, and with a certain degree of justice, of putting the almighty dollar above everything else. One of the objects of this lecture is to make clear that there is something in the world not only higher, but more powerful than money.

As I said in my last lecture, *the idea so prevalent a few years ago in the industrial world that money was the most powerful factor, and that if we only had money enough, nothing else mattered very much, is beginning to lose force, for it is becoming clear that there is an end to the largest bank account, and that the size of the business is not so important as the policy by which it is directed.* Some of our large industrial combinations have already felt the force of this fact, but I doubt very much if those at their heads have a very clear idea of the exact cause of their misfortune.

Too often the system of cost accounting has been to a large extent to blame, for the systems in general use often fail to disclose the real troubles, and content themselves with blaming the shop with inefficiency.

It is true that many shops are managed inefficiently, but it is also true that this inefficiency is often due to financial or selling policies over which the superintendent has no control. As a matter of fact the call for efficiency which has been so loudly proclaimed throughout the country for several years has had a great deal of influence on shop organizations, but *it has hardly been heeded at all in the financial and selling ends of business, where it is needed even worse than in the shops.*

The cost keeping and accounting methods in general use in our industries today are so devised as to put all blame for failure on the producing portion of the business, and do not show the loss due to improper business policies, which it is safe to say are a more fertile source of failure than mistakes made by the production end of the business. I quote from my last lecture: "*A wise policy is of more avail than a large plant; good management than perfect equipment.*"

It is necessary that our cost keeping and accounting methods of the future shall show what losses are due to an unwise policy, or to poor management. In other words, our industrial scheme will not be rounded out until we have a means of measuring the ability with which those at the head of the business perform their functions, that is at least as good as that which we use to measure the efficiency of the operative.

The crying need of such a measure is recognized on all sides, but more especially by those who are engaged in trying to install better methods of management.

A man, who was sent by an independent set of employers to investigate the Lawrence strike, told me that he found much more intelligence among the labor leaders than among the employers concerned, and that they had a far clearer comprehension of the problems involved. His mission in the investigation was to report to those who engaged him as to the best method of combating the I. W. W. They got the answer that nothing permanent could be done until the employers learned more about the industrial problems with which they had to deal.

My experience is that business policies are often as crude as labor policies, but accounting systems as a rule are not so devised as to show such to be the fact.

The time will come, however, and indeed is not far distant, when cost keeping and accounting methods, which in the past have been so devised as to put all blame on the producer, will be so changed as to place blame for failure where it belongs, and give credit to whom credit is due.

Such a change will do much to help the capable workman toward advancement, and will show most clearly the advantage of proper training methods.

Vocational training in the past was acquired through the apprenticeship system, which has apparently broken down under the requirements of modern industrialism. A few years ago it was possible to hire men who had been trained under the apprenticeship system, and the factory manager did not consider it as one of his functions to train workmen, but was in general able to hire, ready trained, the workmen he needed. If he chanced to hire a man who was not suited to the job, he simply discharged him and hired another.

As the number of skilled workmen, who move from place to place, and were in old times known as journeymen, became fewer and fewer, the "hiring and firing" method became less and less satisfactory, until we came face to face with the fact that it too had broken down.

The factory manager is forced, therefore, to accept the responsibility, which undoubtedly is his, of training the workmen he needs, and the question which presents itself to us is how can this best be done. The first method adopted was to allow the "helpers" or "laborers" in a shop to learn from those mechanics with whom they came most in contact, and to promote such of those as seemed to be most capable. Such a system is far from satisfactory, for the method which the helper learns depends largely upon his capacity for imitation, and the ability of the man imitated. A much better method is to select as a trainer or instructor a good workman, who has the proper qualifications for teaching. This produces far better results, for the helper may thus be taught both how to do the work and why it is done.

The best method so far devised is to have the problem studied by a first-class mechanic who is versed in the methods of scientific investigation, and who undertakes to teach the new man the best methods he has been able to devise, the learner being accorded such compensation for success as will induce him to put forth his best efforts.

Because of the fact that in every operation the element of time is an exceedingly important one, and that the only satisfactory method for measuring this element is by means of a stop-watch, the method of investigation in which a stop-watch is used has been called "time study," which gives an erroneous idea of the processes involved. Moreover, as the stop-watch is the only evidence to the ordinary man of what is taking place, many feel, when they have seen an investigator timing an operation, that the work he is doing is very simple, and that they are capable of doing it themselves. They have not seen the planning of the work so that it can be done conveniently and without unnecessary motions or delay, nor do they understand what has been done so that material and tools shall always be ready when wanted by the workmen. They have only seen the stop-watch, which is used to find out how long the workman took. This may bear but little relation to the time he should have taken. In fact the superficial observer usually gets an entirely erroneous idea as to what is going on, and if he undertakes to imitate the work of the trained investigator gets only superficial results.

For instance, if he does not thoroughly understand the work being done, he may carefully time an operation which is absolutely useless, or one which is being done with improper tools. In other words, if the investigator is not thoroughly familiar with the process he is studying, and with the tools or appliances available, his results may be absolutely worthless, in spite of the fact that the operator may have performed the operation very efficiently, or have used the tools most skillfully.

"Efficiency" then, which has been so much advertised, is not the whole answer. To do efficiently something that is not wanted is, of course, better than doing it inefficiently, for some time is saved, good habits are maintained, and the loss is less; but to do the right thing, however inefficiently, will accomplish an end much quicker than doing the wrong thing, however efficiently. This brings us again to the importance of wise direction, or proper leadership. Our ideals must be correct, or our whole scheme of efficiency falls to the ground. Striving efficiently for improper ends may involve all concerned in a catastrophe, the extent of which is measured only by the efficiency with which the end has been striven for.

I intend to make clear in my succeeding lectures that the amount of good work turned out by a factory is of greater importance than any other single item with which the workmen may be concerned. If we can double the output of a factory by paying higher wages, and providing a few extra appliances, we are far better off than if we get the increased output by building an additional factory. Many people do not seem to understand this, and the manager often has an operation studied with a stop-watch, not so much with a view of increasing the output of a man or machine per unit of time, but only with the idea of fixing a proper compensation for the output produced. This has led many people to lay undue emphasis on the use of the stop-watch, and to consider that the sole function of "time study" was to fix a piece rate or set a task.

The term "time study" is most unfortunate, inasmuch as it suggests to many people the idea that getting the time of performing an operation with a stop-watch is necessarily a valuable or important thing. This is often far from a fact. An inexperienced man can draw as many false conclusions from the readings of a stop-watch as from anything else. To make a careful study with a stop-watch of an operation which is being performed improperly is sheer folly, for not only are the results worthless, but the contempt which such a performance naturally stimulates in the mind of an intelligent workman is hard to eradicate. The practice of allowing clerks with stop-watches to go into a factory to study operations about which they are entirely ignorant cannot be too severely condemned. It is this too common practice which is largely responsible for the storm of opposition to the stop-watch on the part of the workmen. When, however, a capable man who has studied a job, and in whose integrity the workmen have confidence, uses a stop-watch in an intelligent manner to get the facts about a piece of work, it is seldom that a workman protests, and even if he does protest, he almost always withdraws his protest when he understands that the investigator is only seeking facts. There are few workmen who do not prefer to have tasks, or even piece rates, based on *facts,* rather than on *guess.* When based on facts, tasks, or piece rates, under any reasonable system of management are permanent; when based on guess, or records, nobody ever expects they will be permanent. The fixing of tasks, or rates, in such a manner is simply laying up trouble for the future.

While the benefit to be derived from the use of a stop-watch in the hands of a capable investigator is undoubtedly great, experience shows that there is far more liability to overestimate the benefit to be derived from its proper use than to foresee the harm that may result from its improper use.

Such improper methods are to a high degree detrimental to the general industrial welfare, for not only do they fail to accomplish the object sought, but they produce in the mind of the workman a suspicion of all methods of investigation, and are apt to cause him to become antagonistic to all employers, much to the detriment of all concerned.

On the other hand, if by a proper study the best method of doing a piece of work has been discovered, and the time it should take a good man to do it determined, nobody is better pleased than the workman, who by this means is taught to do with ease far more work than he ever thought possible. The effect of such training is most marked, and few, who have learned better methods than they knew, are ever willing to go back to the old methods after getting accustomed to the new.

Good habits are often quite as persistent as bad ones, and habits of industry acquired under a proper system of training are a most valuable asset to their possessor. One of the most important industrial problems, then, becomes that of *training workmen in habits of industry,* which are essential for any kind of success.

We all know that when a man becomes interested in his work, it frequently becomes not only the source of his livelihood, but of his amusement as well, and he works at it with unremitting industry. The first step then, in attempting to establish habits of industry, is to make the workman interested in his work. If this can be done, the formation of the proper habits with regard to it follows as a matter of course. The most effective method of stimulating interest in people in general is to set a task, for the accomplishment of which an attractive reward is offered. This seems fundamental, for the earliest form of education given a child is by setting it a task.

The invariable method is to show the child as clearly as possible what is wanted, and then to set a task for it to accomplish. It may be noted that the accomplishment of the task is rendered much easier for both the child and the parent if a suitable reward is offered for its proper performance. As a matter of fact, setting tasks and rewarding performance is the standard method of teaching and training children. The schoolmaster invariably sets tasks, and, while they are not always performed as well as he wishes, he gets far more done than if he had not set them. The college professor finds the task his most effective instrument in getting work out of his students; and, when we in our personal work have something strenuous or disagreeable to accomplish, it is not infrequent that we utilize the same idea to help ourselves, and it does.

The inducement to perform the task is always some benefit or reward. It may not be so immediate as the lump of sugar the child gets, but the work is still done for some reward, immediate or prospective. Further, it is a well-acknowledged fact that to work at a task, which we recognize as being within our power to accomplish without overexerting ourselves, is less tiring and far more pleasant than to work at the same rate with no special goal ahead.

It is simply the difference between working with an object, and without one.

The hunter who enjoys following the trail of the moose, day after day, through snow and bitter cold weather, would find the same traveling very disagreeable except for the task he has set himself. To the uninitiated, golf seems a very inane sort of game, but its devotees work at it with tremendous energy just for the satisfaction of reducing their score a few strokes. As they become more proficient, they become more enthusiastic, for, having performed one task, there is always one just a little harder to work for. A consideration of this subject convinces us that in the vast majority of people there readily springs up the desire to do something specific if the opportunity offers, and if an adequate reward can be obtained for doing it.

The idea of setting for each worker a task with a bonus for its accomplishment seems, then, to be in accord with human nature, and hence the proper foundation for a system of management. Our problem, then, is to find out how to set a proper task and what the reward should be for its accomplishment.

The ideal industrial community would be one in which every member should have his proper daily task and receive a corresponding reward. Such a community would represent the condition of which Kipling says:

> We shall work for an age at a sitting
> and never be tired at all.

This is what modern methods of management are devised to help us accomplish, for under such methods we aim to assign to each, from the highest to the lowest, a definite task each day, and secure to every individual such a reward as will make his task not only acceptable, but agreeable and pleasant.

Under such a system the necessity for driving rapidly disappears, and the development of the best qualities in men goes on apace. Is it not the relative freedom from restrictions and driving methods which makes the Americanized foreigner in a few years so different from his brother in Europe? Opportunity to work for what he conceives to be his own interest, rather than for that of some one else, has undoubtedly a most stimulating effect on a workman.

Was it not this experience that made the American contingent of the Greek army in the Balkan War so superior to the European portion?

A task system, then, which makes a man interested in his work has a beneficial effect far out of proportion to the financial benefits derived.

The task idea is really so common that we do not recognize it. Every railroad schedule consists of a series of tasks, and in the manufacture of such articles as sewing machines, typewriters, and locomotives the task idea is illustrated by the schedules according to which the various parts are started on their way through the different departments, and day by day make such progress as will bring them to the erecting shop at the proper time to be incorporated into the finished machine without delay.

A study of management in general discloses the fact that the "task idea" has held a prominent place in all the most successful systems of management not only of the present, but of the past. The term "task master" is an old one in our language, and symbolizes the time, now happily passing away, when men were compelled to work, not for their own interests, but for those of some one else.

Under a democratic system of government tasks may be set, but the worker must be made to feel that it is to his interest to perform them.

It is safe to say that it is only under a task system of management that the highest development can be reached, and it is our problem therefore to *develop a task system on the basis of democracy that will yield as good, or better, results than those now in operation under autocracy.*

The truest definition of democracy is EQUALITY OF OPPORTUNITY. There is nothing in such democracy that at all conflicts with a task system based on knowledge. In fact the two ideas are completely in harmony, for under the modern task system an effort is made to assign men to the work for which they are best fitted naturally, and to train them to do it efficiently. Our effort then is to approach as nearly as possible that ideal community in which each man shall do the work for which he is best fitted and receive a commensurate reward.

PRINCIPLES OF TASK WORK

III

PRINCIPLES OF TASK WORK

The essential differences between the best systems of today and those of the past are, the manner in which the tasks are set, and the manner in which their performance is rewarded.

To set proper tasks of any kind requires a high degree of knowledge—much higher than even the most capable people engaged in any work usually possess. The result of this condition is, that in the past most tasks have been set by what is called judgment, which is usually another word for *guess*. Even today this method is largely in vogue, for most people have only a vague idea of how to acquire exact knowledge. The usual method is to get together a "committee" of men, often equally ignorant on the subject, and decide by a discussion and a vote. As a method of acquiring knowledge this is about the worst that can be imagined, but I am sorry to say that it is still used even by some educated people.

The result of such a discussion can only be an opinion, which many very good citizens oftentimes cannot distinguish from a fact.

I once asked a successful man what the most important thing was that he learned at college, and promptly got the reply, *the ability to distinguish between an opinion and a fact.* Those of us who have had a scientific training should be able to make this distinction. It is upon us, therefore, that must fall the responsibility for proper guidance of the workman during the transition period, while *fact* is slowly taking the place of *opinion* in industrial affairs.

In most matters concerning materials and forces, the transition has taken place, and the misuse of either is today generally inexcusable; but in matters concerning administration, where the human element is the largest factor, but little has yet been accomplished, and most people still seem to feel that the only way to settle such matters is by consensus of opinion.

There was a time, not very far in the past, when the shape of the earth and the distance of the moon were matters of opinion, and when everybody was ignorant of the nature of fire; but the advance of the scientific method has cleared up most matters of this kind, which have thus been withdrawn from speculation. This, however, is not so with reference to human activities, to which the attention of scientific investigators has only recently been turned. Few people understand the methods of analysis and scientific investigation as applied to human affairs. It is only to be expected, therefore, that any attempt to withdraw this subject from the realm of opinion, and put it into the category of fact, will be opposed by most people, who do not understand the process.

Nevertheless, the scientific study of human activities, and of the capacity of a man for work is making some progress, and it will not be very long before it will be recognized as just as proper a subject of investigation as inanimate materials and forces.

The attempt to substitute scientific knowledge for opinion in the administration of human affairs is what is known as "scientific management," which might better be called "the scientific method in management."

This movement is simply a step in the evolution of industry, and is sure to expand, as the number of scientifically trained men in industry increases. So far scientific management has been looked upon by most people as a specific method; this is far from a fact. It is simply a movement, and the various "systems" that have been devised by leading engineers and others, are simply mechanisms to enable them to give concrete expression to their ideas on the subject.

People are asking what scientific management does. The answer is, "no system ever does anything." It is the man who does things by using one of the mechanisms that has been developed under the name of "scientific management."

The terms "efficiency" and "efficiency engineer," have gained great publicity in the last few years, and we hear much about "personal efficiency." Correspondence school courses are offered for home training. While I am not in sympathy with a great deal of what has been offered under these heads, I believe the net result has been beneficial; but I cannot help feeling that all such isolated efforts will produce only temporary results unless they are based on some fundamentally correct principle.

Too many people are seeking results regardless of how they are obtained, for I have more than once been told that results were wanted, not methods. My reply was, that I was not so much interested in results as in methods, for if we had proper methods the proper results would follow. Men who demand results regardless of methods are largely responsible for the great army of men who call themselves "efficiency engineers," many of whom are not engineers at all, but simply "stunt" peddlers. Nevertheless they are doing some good, for the man who today buys a few valuable stunts, at least learns that he does not possess all available knowledge, and may be led some day to apply the scientific method to his business. Nevertheless, colleges should not cater to such a class, which is already large enough, but should prepare students to grapple with the problem of basing their actions on facts rather than opinions, and thus help train the industrial leaders of the future.

The great problem of the industrial leader is to solve the labor problem. The financier has assumed this task in the past, and the present deplorable conditions are the result. He has failed.

On men such as you must largely fall this task of training future leaders, who have not had the benefit of a college education. To accomplish this you must study all the elements entering into it, of which the human element is the most important.

A recognition of the importance of the human element is quite new. Until recently the engineer had regarded his work done, when he had developed an improved machine or apparatus, and proved by operating it for a short while that its capacity was all he claimed for it. It has then too often been acquired by men imperfectly trained mechanically, but who had the commercial instinct highly developed. Such men usually turn it over to a "cheap" man to operate, and its maintenance is nearly always looked after by a second-rate mechanic, for the commercial man can seldom see why he should have a high-priced man doing repairs.

The efficiency of the machine naturally decreases, and a factory run on these principles must necessarily be more inefficient still.

Fortunately this condition is not universal, for the advantage of having an engineer for a manager has for years been recognized by some, and the number of such is increasing. This number is not sufficiently great, nor has the engineer yet had sufficient training in the art of management to make untrue the statement, which has been so loudly proclaimed recently, that the majority of our industries are very inefficiently managed.

Inasmuch as most factories are controlled by men of commercial instincts or training, their gauge is necessarily not efficiency, of which they know nothing, but profits, of which they know a great deal.

If we would increase the efficiency of a plant, the problem must be put up to a man who knows at least what the word means. Fortunately, the man who knows most about efficiency also knows most, not only about the application of science to the mechanic arts, but also about workmen, by whose side he has obtained his knowledge of and acquired his skill in the use of tools. This man is the engineer. He is the only man who spans the whole gap between the capitalist and the workman, and knows the mental attitude and necessities of each. It is on his shoulders therefore that must fall the burden of harmonizing their interests.

The problem of developing new and better

appliances is not so important today as that of properly utilizing those we have. The recognition of this fact has given rise to the tremendous interest in the subject of management which has become manifest in the last few years. This brings us back again to the training of workmen, for the first thing needed to make any kind of management or administration successful is trained people.

In attempting to train men we must recognize the fact that they are just as susceptible to petty annoyances as their superiors, and that as a rule they are just as anxious to take advantage of any opportunities that are afforded them, if they are benefited by so doing. No sooner do we, as a rule, afford opportunities for men to show their ability and to advance themselves than some begin to come to the front. We must not, however, expect by any system of management to produce a revolution. If we can put in a system by which the workman is benefited and enabled to utilize his powers to better advantage, although he will gradually appreciate it, we must not expect him to do so at once. His experience in the past has taught him that his employer has usually but little interest in his advancement, and will give him only such compensation as he is forced to give. Having lived under such a condition for years, which is necessarily one of antagonism for his employer, time must always elapse before he will believe that the opportunities apparently offered him are real.

If, however, the work is done under a properly trained engineer, who recognizes the advantages of co-operation, and is willing to share them with the workman, we have no difficulty in ultimately bringing him to a proper frame of mind.

Our difficulty in the past has been mainly with the commercial man, who has certain theories of efficiency gained from the cost accountant which are fatal to our efforts to make improvements of any kind.

Of these theories, there are two which have stood most prominently in the way of anything looking to the advancement of the workman. The first, which is, fortunately, coming to be discredited, is that *in order to get low costs the expense of the supervising force must be small compared to that of those who are actually performing the physical work.* This ratio has for a long time been held by many accountants to be a measure of efficiency. The result of this theory is that the foreman or superintendent who wishes to make a good showing in the eyes of the cost accountant has as large a pay roll as possible in order that the ratio of his salary and that of his clerks to the wages of the workmen may be small. I have known foremen who objected to having their force reduced because they would be criticised for making a poorer showing. The other fallacy, viz., *that it is necessary to have low wages in order to have low costs,* is equally detrimental to all concerned. Inasmuch as it is far easier, as a rule, to criticise a pay roll than it is to criticise the amount of work done by the people on that pay roll, the man in authority oftentimes concentrates his efforts on keeping down the pay roll, regardless of the amount of work done, which he has made no provision to measure.

The usual method of holding down the pay roll is to see that no man makes more than a very moderate wage. Under such management men invariably do only a very moderate amount of work, and the effort on the part of the manager to see how little money can be spent usually has the effect of causing a correspondingly small amount of work to be done.

These two theories, which perhaps have done more to hold back the advancement of our industries than any other causes, are gradually becoming discredited. The increasing productivity of our automatic machinery, which requires but little direct labor, but oftentimes quite a good deal of supervision, has discredited one of them, and the recognized efficiency of the well-paid, high-grade workman is rapidly doing away with the other.

The fact that modern industrialism is rapidly bringing into discredit his two pet theories is seriously disconcerting to the average accountant, who has been successful as the principal adviser of the financier in commercial activities, for which his methods were developed. He now begins to realize that there is a radical difference between trade and industry, and that the methods of accounting, which were valuable in the former case, may be worthless in the latter. In commerce, or trade, the comptroller and the accountant are indeed extremely important people; for when the ships of Holland and England brought the surplus silks of

India and China to Europe, it mattered little to the merchant who produced the goods, but it was extremely important that the finances should be properly safeguarded. When, however, two rival producers today bid for the privilege of supplying locomotives to a railroad, we have an entirely different state of affairs; the producer now becomes the important man and the accountant primarily his record keeper. Inasmuch as modern manufacturing developed out of the necessities of the older form of trade, we should not be surprised to find that it has inherited habits and beliefs that should long ago have become obsolete. The most serious of these is the fact that the financier, in many cases, still sincerely believes the accountant to be more important than the manufacturer, even though he only keeps a record of what the manufacturer does.

It is a great shock, therefore, to both the financier and the accountant, to realize that the ancient and honorable position of comptroller is beginning to lose under modern manufacturing methods, the relative importance it acquired when physical labor was not esteemed as it now is, and when hewers of wood and drawers of water were held in contempt.

Now, however, that labor is held to be honorable, and the man who knows what to do and how to do it is claiming an equal place with him who knows what was done and who did it, we recognize that it is time we readjusted the traditional relative positions of the record keeper and the doer.

The record keeper is just as essential as ever, but under modern methods he must yield his supremacy to the producer, and give up his privilege of being simply a critic.

An accountant, as a rule, feels that he has done his duty when he, after two or three months, brings to the president his criticisms of the factory. Such an accountant is really a "non-producer," and there is no place for him in modern manufacturing. What is needed is a man who will keep the records up to date, and furnish the superintendent, day by day if necessary, with an exact account of the money spent and the work done. Such a man is not a "non-producer" but a great help to the superintendent.

In the modern factory, there is no room for the "non-producers," everybody must help, or he has no place; the accountant as an assistant to the superintendent takes on a new dignity as a producer.

He no longer regards the ratio of indirect to direct labor as important, but co-operates with the superintendent to reduce their *sum*, and for this purpose is glad to reduce either, or both, regardless of the effect on the ratio.

Until these fundamental ideas are fully comprehended and acquiesced in, it is not possible to establish a successful system of task work.

The reason why tasks or piece rates have been, to a large extent, unsatisfactory in the past, is because they have been based on what has been done, or somebody's *opinion* of what could be done, instead of *exact knowledge* of what could be done. Capable workmen, who exceeded the past records, or the amount which had been decided upon by the opinion of those in charge, were almost always penalized for their extra efforts by having their compensation reduced, or their task increased. This method of dealing with workmen had been in vogue for many years, and the industrial relations between employer and employee were rapidly becoming worse and worse, due largely to the fact that the method of compensation of the workmen had no fixed basis.

It was this fact that first aroused the late Dr. Frederick Winslow Taylor, who early in his career concluded that if progress was to be made in directing human activities, that direction must be founded neither on records of past performance, nor on the opinion of any man as to what should be done, but on *knowledge* of the matter concerned. It was painful to him to see a group of people discussing a subject about which they were equally ignorant, and deciding the question by vote. The great work of his life was a battle with such methods, and the triumph of the scientific method over the debating society as a means of establishing a basis for action on questions involving the interest of employers and employees, is his great contribution to the world's work.

The development of a method of treating steel, which gave him great prominence at the time, and which has so frequently been referred to, of the system of management that bears his name, and of the successful prosecution of the various activities with which his name has been associated, are but incidents in his career, and only the logical outcome of his determination to advance the sum of human knowledge on all subjects in which he became interested—this he never failed to do.

It is his substitution of the scientific method of determining what can be done as a basis for action, instead of records of what had been done, or opinion of what can be done, that marks the new industrial spirit, with which I hope to inspire you.

Modern industrial management aims to set a task for each member of the organization from the highest to the lowest, but task setting in its ordinarily accepted sense is not the first problem that confronts us. An industrial institution today is a large co-operative undertaking. Before we can ask people to perform tasks, which we know are well within their ability, if they have available the proper materials and appliances, it is necessary for us to provide such an organization as will furnish them with the materials and appliances needed to perform those tasks.

While it is impossible for me in a course of this nature to go into the general problem of administration, and to describe to you a mechanism which enables us to accomplish the object we have in mind, it must be perfectly evident that certain things are necessary. For instance, we must always be able to supply the workmen with the materials and equipment needed before we ask him to perform his task. To do this we must know in advance what is to be done each day, and not only that the materials on which he is to work are on hand, but that the equipment which he needs is not in use for some other purpose. It is not easy to establish in a large organization a system of management which can insure such condition of affairs; but before we can pretend to ask people to perform regularly tasks which we may assign to them, such an organization must be in good working condition. To develop such an organization and to get it in smooth working order involves a great deal of work and time, and oftentimes the changing of the viewpoint and duties of many members of the staff.

This problem can seldom be accomplished to such a degree as to warrant our beginning to set tasks in less than a year, and more often it takes nearly two years.

It is very important that this be thoroughly understood, and also that there is but little chance of success for a young man who equips himself with a stop-watch and calls himself an "efficiency engineer" unless he has mastered this part of the subject.

Proper task setting itself is not nearly so simple an operation as most people think.

Before we begin to study an operation in detail with the object of setting a task we must ask

1st—Is the operation necessary?

2d—Is it being done in the best manner?

When these are answered, other detail questions follow.

To answer these questions at all requires a knowledge of the work to be done and of the equipment available, which rules out at once the clerk with a stop-watch.

Many unnecessary operations are being done in almost every shop. In many cases these operations were once necessary, but when changes were made, it was not realized that they were no longer necessary, and the habit of performing them continued. The first duty therefore of the task setter is to answer the first question and establish the fact that the operation is necessary before he begins to study it.

To answer the second question satisfactorily it is necessary to have an extensive knowledge of shop methods and appliances, for it is the height of absurdity to study carefully an operation which is being done by the wrong method or with inferior appliances. Having decided that an operation is necessary, and that it is being done by the best appliances available, the next question is—Are the appliances being used as efficiently as possible?

It is at this point that the knowledge and experience of the investigator are most put to the test, for even though using the same methods and appliances there may be a great deal of difference in the time taken and the quality of the product.

Having decided upon the proper method of using the appliances and the time needed to turn out a product of a proper quality, the next question often is, "Are there any other appliances that it would pay us to make or to buy to turn out the product quicker or better?"

Before we can finally decide upon the proper method and time for performing an operation, we often have to answer not only these questions, but a host of others concerning the details of the operations involved.

Having decided upon a reasonable time for performing the operation (which time is measured by a stop-watch) the next problem is to teach the operative to perform it in that time.

Inasmuch as any large reduction in the time of an operation is usually made by a change in method, it is necessary to get the operator out of his old habits and to train him in the new ones.

A habit has been likened to a rut, and the analogy is a good one, for we must not only get a wheel out of the old rut, but we must fill the rut up if we wish to be sure that the wheel will not get into it again. It is just so with the workman and the habit; we must make it impossible for him to fall back into his old habit, or we have no assurance at all that he will continue in the new.

In order to explain more specifically the method of studying an operation and the effect produced, I wish to call your attention to Chart I, which is the study of a girl operating a sewing machine. You will note from this that the average time taken on the operation by the best girl previous to the beginning of the study was 2.17 minutes. The girl whose operation it was decided to study was not the fastest girl in the room, yet during the first day she averaged 1.6

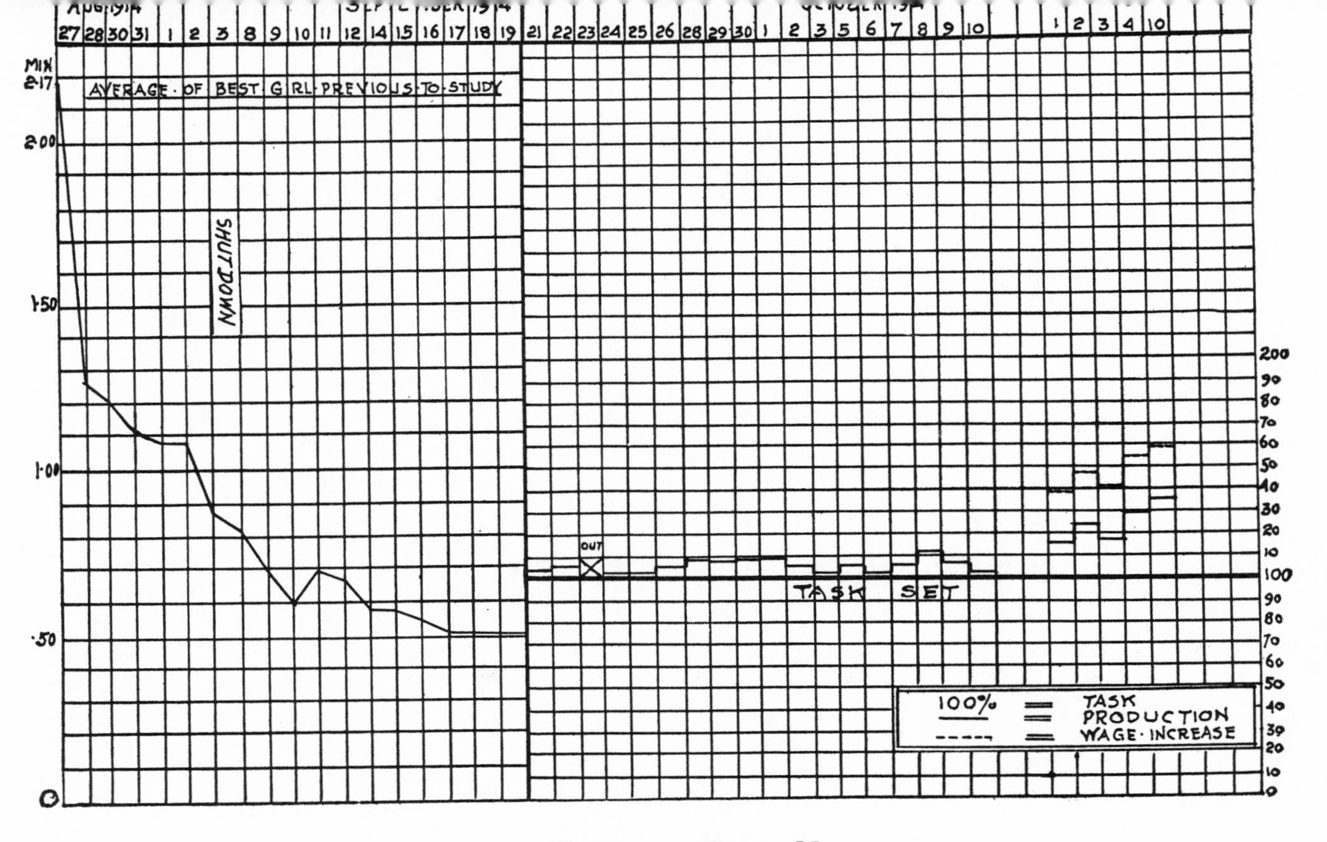

CHART I. HEMMING ON SEWING-MACHINE.

minutes per operation. You naturally ask what caused this change? There were several elements which effected it.

1. Before we began to study the operation nobody had given special attention to the method of supplying the girls with work, and they were often compelled to waste time waiting for work to do.

2. When the work was brought to them, it was seldom placed in a position which made the handling of it convenient or easy.

3. Each of the girls in the room was working on several different operations during the day, and oftentimes needed different colored thread. When we began to study this subject we planned to have fewer changes in the jobs the girls were doing so that when any girl had her machine prepared for any one class of work she did all of that work available.

Simply doing these things produced quite a marked reduction in the time needed, and for several days the amount of time needed to perform the work gradually decreased.

On September 19th a task was set for this operation, and the time allowed was represented by the distance from the zero line to the heavy horizontal line beginning at the line of September 19th.

The position of this line shows that the time allowed was 30 per cent greater than the time actually taken by the girl during the last few days of study.

Representing, now, the amount of work to be done to accomplish the task as the distance from the zero line to the heavy horizontal line, the irregular line above the heavy line represents the amount of work done each day, which although varying from day to day, exceeded the task on October 8th by about 12 per cent. Further to the right on the same chart is shown the production on the same task during the early days of the following March, which on March 10th exceeded 30 per cent of the task.

The compensation for the performance of the task in the time allowed, or less, was pay at the day rate for the time allowed plus 25 per cent of that time.

In the early days of the following March this compensation amounted to 50 per cent over the day rate. This is also represented on the same chart by the dashed line, the day rate being the 100 per cent line.

You will note on Chart II, which repre-

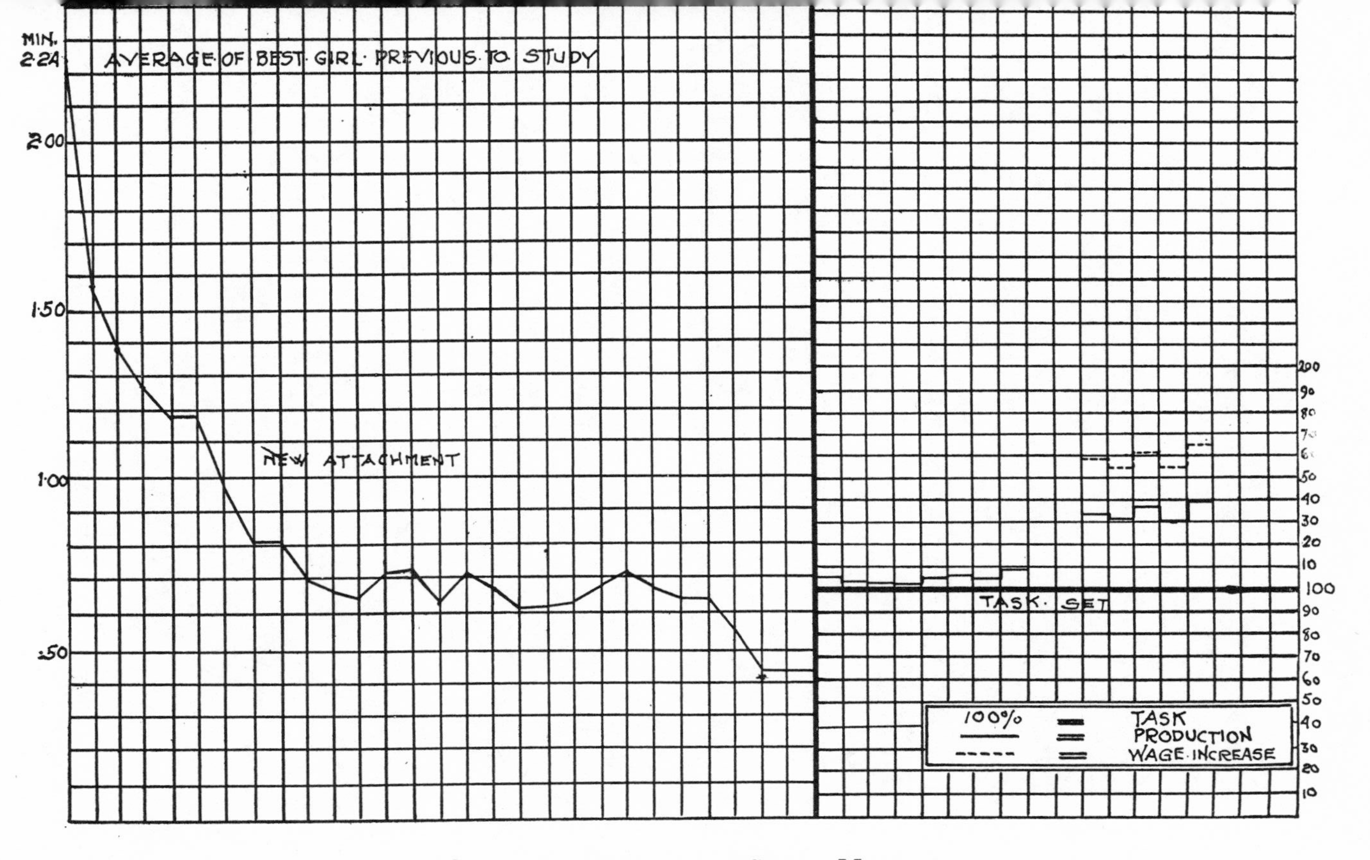

CHART II. OPERATING ON SEWING-MACHINE.

sents a similar study of another sewing machine operation, a downward curve of almost the same shape. While the operative was getting accustomed to doing the best she could under new conditions, it was the business of the task setter to find what other conditions were hampering her. The improved conditions which the investigator was able to establish enabled the operative in four or five days to make another marked reduction in the time. When all the improvements that it seemed likely the investigator could devise had been made, and the time of performing the operation had been accordingly reduced, the task was set, allowing about 30 per cent more time to do the work than it had been clearly demonstrated was necessary. As in diagram No. I, the heavy line represents the time allowed for the task according to the scale at the left of the chart. The distance from zero to the task line may be made to represent the number of pieces to be done in a unit of time (the task). The distance from the zero line to the line above the task line shows the number of pieces, compared with the task as a unit, that were done each day by the operator. This line shows that the operator exceeded the task sometimes nearly 10 per cent, even when the task was new. This excess by the middle of the following March became as much as 40 per cent, and the wages over 60 per cent in addition to the day rate. This is shown as on Chart I.

These two charts are fair examples of investigation and task setting methods, and the results shown are normal results.

If it is desired to accomplish such results the investigator must not be a clerk with a stop-watch, but a man competent to study problems and to draw correct conclusions from his studies. He must also be a good teacher with an abundance of patience, for the formation of new habits of work is a slow process.

Every case of failure to perform the task successfully must be investigated and the cause removed. This would be impossible if tasks were so severe that any little trifle would cause failure. Hence, the time allowed for the performance of a task must be liberal enough to enable a good workman to exceed it by a fair margin, in order that any little unusual occurrence may not cause failure, and keep our foremen and investigators busy with trifles. On the other hand, the *best work* is invariably gotten when the task is severe enough to command for its proper performance the undivided attention of the operator.

One of the greatest benefits of the task system is that, when properly operated, it compels this very thing, and trains workers to keep their minds on what they are doing. A disclosure of this fact often brings the protest that too close attention to a job is detrimental to the health of the operative. The reply is that close attention is not nearly so tiring as trying to do something the mind is not on, which under the usual conditions is too often the case. All bonus workers recognize this fact, and many have expressed themselves as being less tired at the end of the day when working on task work, than they were before task work was started, and when they were doing much less work.

As a matter of fact *doing absolutely nothing* is quite as tiring as working very hard, so that it is only reasonable that a worker may often increase his speed materially and be less tired at the end of the day, as we actually find to be the case.

As a further substantiation of this fact there is always a distinct improvement in the health and cheerfulness in workers after they begin doing task work. This is particularly noticeable in the case of girls, who soon begin to take more pride in their personal appearance.

The full effect of this work is seen not only in the improved appearance of the workers, but in the general appearance of the shop, the whole tone of which rapidly improves.

RESULTS OF TASK WORK

IV

RESULTS OF TASK WORK

The objections brought by many against all forms of task work are based on a misconception of the task idea as applied to modern industry. The task master of the past was practically a slave driver, whose principal function was to force workmen to do that which they had no desire to do, or interest in doing. The task setter of today under any reputable system of management is not a driver. When he asks the workmen to perform tasks, he makes it to their interest to accomplish them, and is careful not to ask what is impossible or unreasonable.

A little consideration will show that such a policy is only in accord with common sense, and that the policy of insisting that a man shall do a thing, when we do not know whether he can do it or not, is, to say the least, not productive of the best results. Nevertheless, such a policy has been so common in the past that it is extremely difficult to make the workman really believe that we disapprove of it, for he has seldom had any such experience. Indeed, many employers, who are trying to follow the newer ideals, still believe down in their hearts that the newer method is in reality not as much to their interest as the old. Until they have had sufficient time to demonstrate to themselves the superiority from a financial standpoint of the newer method over the old, many who have not given the subject thorough study will insist on more or less of a mixture of the two methods. As long as there is even a suspicion of the older method in connection with the newer, the workman is certainly not to be condemned for his hesitation in accepting it. When, however, proper methods have been used to determine how work should be done and to set tasks, the workman becomes impressed with the sincerity of the task setters and instructors, and it is not long before he is willing to co-operate, provided the compensation for so doing is attractive enough. As a matter of fact the gain to the employer in having the operator turn out a maximum quantity of the best grade of work is so great that it is decidedly to his interest to compensate the worker with sufficient liberality to induce him to co-operate. To secure the co-operation of the worker, however, is not the whole solution, for it is seldom possible for the ordinary worker without training to keep his attention fixed sufficiently well on his work to perform properly a reasonable task, unless an effort is made by the instructor to help do so. It is not only necessary to instruct the worker in the physical motions necessary to perform his task, but to train him to perform them without waste of time. This requires mental concentration on the part of the worker, and one of the most valuable results of task work, as far as the worker is concerned, is the formation of habits of concentration by which he keeps his mind on what he is doing, and invariably produces more and better work with less fatigue.

Speed of working is largely a matter of habit, and, within reasonable limits, does not greatly affect the amount of fatigue produced.

Idling, or working very slowly, is quite as tiring as excessive speed, and much more demoralizing. There is a rate of working which seems to be most beneficial to the health and spirits of the workers, and we have a good deal of evidence to show that this rate is much faster than that at which people as a rule work. Our task workers are invariably more cheerful and enjoy better health than day workers on the same work.

The one stumbling-block that seems to stand in the way of the general acceptance of the task idea is that it is supposed that tasks are set without the co-operation of the worker. As a matter of fact it is extremely difficult to set a task without the co-operation of the operative, and absolutely to the detriment of the employer to set a task that cannot be performed regularly. To say, however, as some contend, that the amount of work a man should do, should be decided as the result of an argument between the task setter and the workman is absurd, for the amount of work a man can do is discoverable only by the methods of scientific investigation, and few workers have ever had any experience with such methods. The task can be decided correctly only by people who have learned the scientific method of making investigations and determining facts. Moreover, there are involved in this question, principles that are both moral and economic.

First: *We have no right morally to*

decide as a matter of opinion that which can be determined as a matter of fact.

Second: *If we allow ourselves to be governed by opinion where it is possible to obtain facts, we shall lose in our competition with those who base their actions on facts.*

The substitution of fact for opinion is the basis of modern industrial progress, and the rate of this progress is controlled by the extent to which the methods of scientific investigation supplant the debating society methods in determining a basis for action.

A man basing his actions on knowledge, or facts, is in a far more secure position than he who has only opinion for his guide, and is likely to get the best of his competitors, who base their actions on opinions.

We must realize in discussing all such questions that the law of the *survival of the fittest* not only applies to men as well as to plants and animals, but to corporations and nations. Protection of whatever sort (and this includes combinations to uphold prices) is an expedient to prevent the operation of this law, and hence can be only temporary in its effect, for in the long run individuals, corporations, and nations must conform to the working of that inexorable law.

The great war now devastating Europe is making it increasingly clear that we are living in an industrial age, and that efficient industrialism is no longer second to efficient militarism. The man at the lathe is just as potent a factor now as the man behind the gun. If we try to regulate the output of the shop by agreements or arbitration we are bound to fall before him who scientifically establishes an ideal (a proper task) and consistently strives for its attainment.

The idea that we can neutralize the operation of a natural law by agreement is only seriously held by those who do not understand clearly what a natural law is, and that nation whose people individually and as a whole strive most intelligently to conform to natural laws, will in the long run establish its superiority.

The war is making clear the fact that productive efficiency is the greatest force not only in industry, but in war, and hence *an idle class, whatever its excuse, is a serious handicap to any nation.*

The idea that the acquisition of wealth should confer upon us immunity from labor, is fast giving away before the feeling that wealth should give us the opportunity to work at that which we can do best, and thereby enable us to increase our productive efficiency.

It is a fact that present industrial conditions in this country are unsatisfactory, and in order to find out if it may not be possible to pass laws to alleviate them, Congress in the spring of 1914 authorized the appointment of a commission to investigate the industrial conditions and to recommend legislation.

No matter how we may criticise the present commission, we cannot deny that the attempt to find a way out of our present industrial difficulties is a laudable one. I do not feel, however, that the result is to come primarily through legislation, but by recognition on the part of employer and employee that there is a possible basis for mutual understanding, and that it is our duty to find it. Such a basis cannot be discovered by bodies of men resolving themselves into debating societies, but must be found by a thorough investigation by the scientific method of the industrial conditions as they exist.

It is undoubtedly the duty of the government to afford protection to the people as a whole and individually, and to guarantee to each, as far as possible, an equal opportunity for the pursuit of fortune, health, and happiness. Such being the case, it is undoubtedly a function of the government to see that no undue advantage is taken of one citizen by another, or by a corporation; and hence it must investigate the operation of the various systems of management that are being so extensively advertised. In order to co-operate with the government in this laudable undertaking, employers should keep such records as will show the kind of treatment their workmen are receiving, and the effect of such treatment on their financial and physical well-being. In an industrial community, it is a proper function of the government to ask how workmen are being compensated and how the work they are doing is affecting their health and happiness.

We have to a large measure furnished the answer to these questions by keeping an individual daily record of each workman. Many will claim that the keeping of such records imposes a hardship on the employer and is a source of unnecessary expense. My experience is quite the contrary. In a properly organized shop there is no difficulty for one worker to keep such a record for from

50 to 100 employees, thus making the cost of keeping the record not over 2 per cent of the total wages. Such records, if used by the foreman or superintendent to study the shop conditions, invariably show him why work has not been accomplished, and point out many easily removable obstacles. As a matter of fact, such records are usually quite as effective in enabling the foreman to perform his functions more intelligently as they are as a stimulus to the individual workman. Keeping them invariably results in a decided increase in output, often reaching 15 to 20 per cent, which is a very good return for the 2 per cent increase in the pay roll. I said, however, in recommending this method that it could be applied in a properly organized shop. I wish further to state that *if it cannot be applied to any advantage, it is generally evidence that the shop is not properly organized.*

Under our task system of management we have made provision for just this sort of thing. Our red and black charts show us daily which of our workers have succeeded in performing the tasks assigned to them and which have failed. A daily report of the failures with the reasons therefor, and what has been done to obviate such failures in the future, complete the daily record. These red and black charts are kept up indefinitely and are designed to show what becomes of all the workmen who worked under these methods, for on each chart opposite the proper operative is noted any change in his occupation; or if he discontinues this work, why it was discontinued. Several such charts have been published in my book, "WORK, WAGES AND PROFITS," so there is no need for reproducing all of them here, but for illustration I will reproduce two or three:

Chart No. III represents the bonus work of girls "burling" cloth in a worsted mill. Burling consists of mending defects in the cloth, pulling knots to the back side of the cloth, &c.

On this chart, No. III, the numbers of the operatives are placed on the left-hand side and the line opposite each operative represents her record. The vertical lines represent days, and the heavy vertical lines represent weeks. A black mark covering the space of any day represents that the worker performed her task on that day and earned her bonus. A red mark means that she failed to perform her task, and got only her day rate. A red cross means that she was absent. A black cross means she was not doing task work.

Of course, after setting the task we gave the best operatives in the room the first opportunity to work upon it, and you will note that they earned their bonus quite regularly, failure occurring most often on Saturday. On the 16th of March you will note that they had a dance, and that there was considerable failure on that account. It seems that with girls there is usually failure just before an important event and also afterwards.

If you follow this chart across you will note what became of the various operatives—in the next few months one was made an instructor, one was made a clerk, and one entered a convent.

The first tasks in this room were set on February 7th, and, as I said before, given to the best operators. We made a list of all the operators in the room and assigned tasks to them in the order of their excellence as shown by past records. Although all the work in this room was of exactly the same nature, we did not get all the girls on task work until the middle of July.

You will note how much more frequently the poorer girls failed to perform their tasks, but you will also notice the quite rapid improvement which was made by the poorer girls after we assigned one of the better girls to the duty of instructing them.

There were 161 girls in this room. The chart shows the record of the best and of the poorest girls. You will note that on the last day all those shown on this chart earned bonus. The improvement in the work of the poorer girls during the months of June and July is very marked.

Chart No. IV represents girls winding yarn in a cotton mill. This chart, as well as the one I have just shown, I have used a number of times for the reason that they both illustrate certain facts very clearly. Chart No. IV is one of the first charts which I kept, and I did not begin to keep it until the task work had been in operation for some little time. It represents our progress in training workers to do their tasks in winding weaving bobbins—bobbins of filling that go into the shuttles. Each operative tends a number of spindles, and the work consists first of taking out full bobbins and putting empty ones in place; and second, of removing empty spools from which the yarn has been taken, and replacing them with full spools. Inasmuch as the machine runs at a constant speed, the bobbins fill and the spools empty more rapidly with coarse yarn than with fine; hence it was necessary to make a careful detail study of the subject to set a proper task for different sizes of yarn. This study took about six weeks, and, having settled upon proper tasks, we started a girl named Wagner on task work early in February. She would not do it at first but stayed home a week. At the end of that time she came to work, willing to do as we wished, and was evidently surprised at the ease with which she succeeded. On March 1 we began to keep the charts. At that time those doing the task as shown by the chart represented but a small proportion of the whole number of workers. Our gang boss, McCabe, received 5 cents for each worker that made a bonus and 10 cents each if all made it. Our task setter was constantly on hand at first, to help him remove obstacles, and to see that the workers had every opportunity to work efficiently. In spite of this, a large proportion of the first ones failed to earn the bonus regularly and gradually left. Many of these were evidently girls, who found continuous attention to their work irksome, and, even though they were capable of doing the work, preferred the more free and easy method to which they had been accustomed. Others showed but little ability to do the work or to learn. The fact, however, which is evident from the chart—that the larger the number of *bonus workers* in the mill, the faster the new ones learned—is a matter of great psychological importance. *There is in every workroom a fashion, a habit of work, and the new worker follows that fashion, for it isn't respectable not to.*

The man or woman who ignores fashion does not get much pleasure from associating with those that follow it, and the new member consequently tries to fall in with the sentiment of the community. Our chart shows that the stronger the sentiment in favor of industry is, the harder the new worker tries and the sooner he succeeds. We must therefore make our compensation such as to encourage the habit, or fashion, of industry; our charts show to what extent we have succeeded in fixing this habit.

It is interesting to note that although

failures most frequently occurred on Monday; even this habit could be cured.

The mill shut down for about three days around July 4 to take stock, and as we had just gotten this room in good shape, that little vacation may be used as a dividing line on this chart. Remembering that solid black indicates that the full amount of work has been done, and that all of it was up to standard for quality, while solid red represents that the work was below standard either for quantity or quality, and sometimes for both, also that the black cross means the worker was doing day work, while the red cross means that the worker was absent, the amount of solid black on any day is a measure of efficiency for that day and the red is a very accurate measure of the amount of supervision needed, for all cases of failure to perform the task must be investigated, and all cases of absenteeism should be inquired into. The gradual change of the chart from red to black means not only that the workers are becoming more skillful and regular in their habits, but that the machinery is being kept in better order, for the task is so set that unless the machines are in good condition the bonus cannot be earned.

After July 4, not only was the amount of supervision needed diminished and a regular output maintained, but the workers were much more regular in attendance. The indications of the chart are that the output of the room after July 4 was larger, better, and more uniform. It is now easy to predict the daily output and to make promises of delivery that will be kept without effort on the part of the foreman. Before July 4 such predictions were only estimates, and a proper output could not be kept up even by constant supervision. As the gang boss in this room gets a bonus of 5 cents for each worker who earns a bonus, and 10 cents each if all earn bonus, it is easy to see that the superintendent does not have to worry much about the quantity or quality of the product. It is easy to measure the quantity, and the quality is taken care of through the payment of a bonus for quality to the foreman.

By permission of the treasurer of this mill I am enabled to show Chart V representing the conditions in this room in 1912, three years later. The preponderance and continuity on this chart of black spaces showing task performed are very marked.*

*At present writing (1915) the chart is blacker than in 1912.

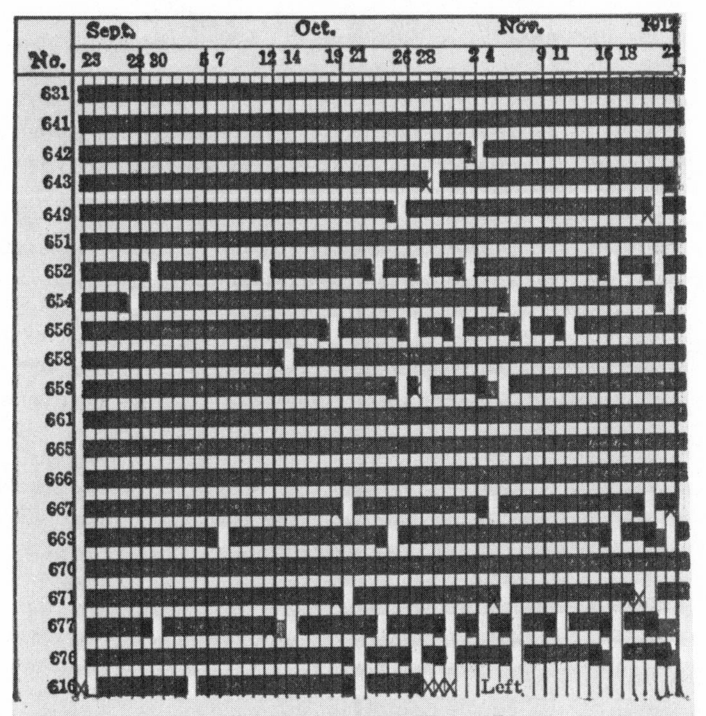

CHART V. BONUS RECORD, THREE YEARS LATER, OF FILLING WINDERS' DEPARTMENT SHOWN IN CHART IV.

Reproduced by courtesy of *The Engineering Magazine*, publishers of "Work, Wages and Profits," by H. L. Gantt.

0 20 40 60 80 100 150 200 250 300

Date	Job
6-27-14	PP 98U 27190
7-3-14	PP116U 52670
7-15-14	PP69B 30060
7-16-14	PP118U 20670 20671
7-23-14	PP120U 28820
7-31-14	PP123U 12412
9-23-14	PP125U 12190
9-24-14	PP126U 12200
1-11-15	PP62U 90160
1-26-15	PP99B 30080
2-18-15	PP154U 14260
2-22-15	PP89B 14260
2-24-15	PP14T 14260
2-27-15	PP156U 14260
3-2-15	PP63A 51540
3-3-15	PP77F 14260
3-5-15	PP54A 51690
3-5-15	PP54A 25640
3-9-15	PP1A 53691 57250
3-11-15	PP82U 26420
3-11-15	PP95U 26441
3-12-15	PD51R 13796
3-13-15	PP71U 26442
3-15-15	PP48U 26440
3-16-15	PP112B 14260
3-16-15	PP126U 26425
3-17-15	PP42B 64060
3-17-15	PP42B 64110
3-18-15	PP42B 65471
3-18-15	PP160U 27345
3-20-15	PP 42B 64840
3-22-15	PP68U 55933
3-23-15	PP64A 51540
3-24-15	PP162U 26432
3-25-15	PP115B 55950
3-25-15	PD51R 13773
3-25-15	PP116B 12170
3-27-15	PP165U 26423
3-31-15	PP51C 14352
4-1-15	PP65A 35520
4-2-15	PP164U 36012

SHEPHERD

CHART VI. TASK PERFORMANCE AND WAGES ON PUNCH-PRESS WORK.

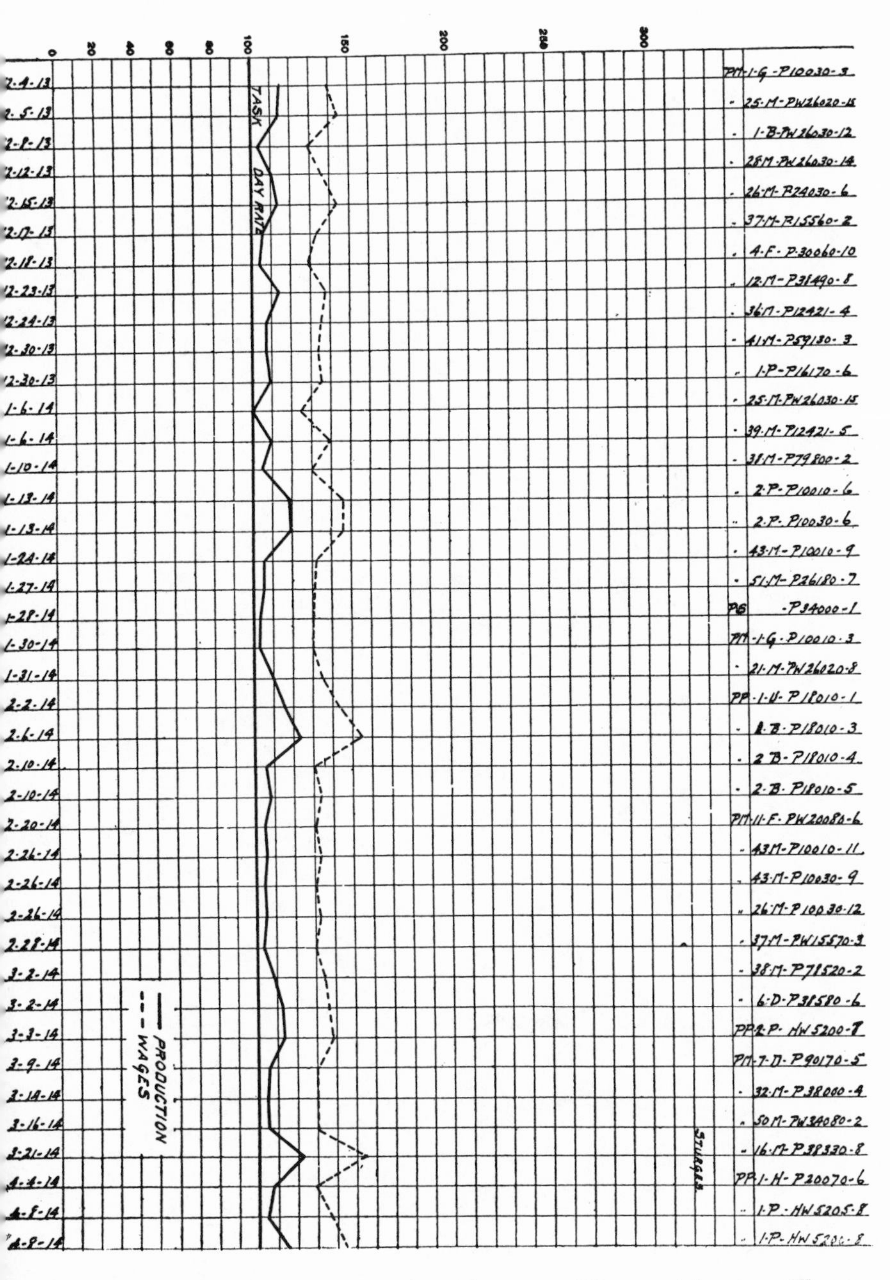

CHART VII. TASK PERFORMANCE AND WAGES ON MILLING-MACHINE WORK.

These charts are typical and we have many others showing similar results, the most pronounced of which are an improvement in skill and regularity in attendance.

Among the questions which the Commission on Industrial Relations asks are:

How do the wages of the task workers compare with those of day workers in the same community, and are the task workers not continually under a strain in attempting to perform their tasks?

Charts VI and VII from different shops answer these questions. The heavy black line marked 100 represents the amount of the task. The symbol at the top of each vertical line indicates the kind of work, and the date at the bottom when the task was set.

On each vertical line is shown the result of a separate task, the heavy irregular line showing the average amount of work done on the various tasks after the worker had gotten used to the work. It will be noted that the performance line is seldom less than 10 per cent above the task, and often much higher. In other words the workers are easily exceeding their task.

These charts also show the ratio of the wages earned by the operatives as compared to their day rates, which are the normal day rates of the community.

Representing the distance from the zero line to the heavy black (100 per cent) line as the day rate, the broken line represents the average earnings on the corresponding tasks, showing a marked increase over the day rate.

These charts then would seem to answer all the questions which any one would care to ask about such work, except the one question which seems to agitate many people to a far greater extent than any other—Does not such a system of management tend to make machines of the operatives? This can best be answered by studying the red and black charts over a long period and noting the unusually large percentage of the workers who are advanced to more important positions. As a matter of fact, after we have established such a system of management the problem of securing trained people for the higher positions gives us but little further trouble, for we find among our task workers people who are rapidly fitting themselves to fill the higher positions, and the practice of going outside of the organization to hire a foreman or an inspector is soon given up.

Many times I have been told on undertaking work with a new concern, that they had no capable men to draw upon for filling important positions, and have had the same people tell me at the end of a few years that they were no longer being troubled by that difficulty. Many employers who have desired to promote their own workmen to the higher positions have been unable to do so because they had no system of training which fitted their employees for the positions to be filled. Such employers have been quick to grasp the possibilities of our training methods, and are no longer dependent upon outside help. Not only does this system of training furnish us with foremen and others whose work is directly connected with that of the workmen, but if our operatives have a fair school education it furnishes us with by far the best corps of clerks and storekeepers which we can obtain, and oftentimes good task setters.

There is a feeling in the mind of every young man that it is an advance for him to go from the shop to the office, and it is certainly a great advantage to the office to have clerks who are familiar with the actual work in the shop.

In many quarters I find that there is a serious objection on the part of the management to use shop-trained men as clerks on the plea that such men demand higher wages than the clerks who have had no shop experience. This is undoubtedly true, but the work they do is worth a great deal more than if it were done by somebody to whom the names of the things with which he was dealing were only words, and the numbers he was using only figures. Not only are these shop-trained clerks far more valuable than those that are simply office trained, but the stimulus which the men in the shop get by having their fellows advance is quite worth all the costs.

Capable shopmen who advance through the clerical end to important positions get a much broader view of the business than if their experience has been only in one branch.

College men who have had a pretty liberal shop experience become rapidly available for important work if their advance is by this method.

Experience as timekeepers and production clerks is the best training I have been yet able to devise to fit a man for task setting; for to become a good task setter he must be familiar with the timekeeping and production systems that are needed for a task system of management.

It is therefore well in any organization adopting the task system of management to have time and production clerks of such education as will enable them to become task setters if they develop the proper ability.

PRODUCTION AND SALES

V

PRODUCTION AND SALES

In my former lectures I have not only tried to impress upon you the importance of leadership in industrial affairs; but to give you an idea of how industrial leaders may be developed and trained for the direction of our industries in the production of wealth and the increase in happiness of our people. This leads us, naturally, to the broad subject of production.

A nation's wealth depends ultimately on its powers of production. Buying and selling articles within a nation transfers such articles from one ownership to another, but such changes in ownership do not increase the amount of wealth, although they may put it in more available form. Iron ore in the earth is worth very little; the same ore *mined* and *transported* to the blast furnace is much more valuable; changed into pig iron it becomes more valuable still; changing the iron into steel still further increases its value; finally the hairspring for a watch made from this steel is worth more per ounce than the ore in the earth was per ton.

The progressive increase of value is due to human labor. The cost of the various transitions through which the iron ore has passed before it becomes a watch spring depends upon the intelligence and efficiency with which that human labor has been applied. The object of all of our industrial efforts is to transform comparatively cheap raw materials into valuable products. The central idea of all industry, therefore, is *production* and all our efforts should be bent on producing as efficiently as possible.

This is a very different condition from merchandizing, in which the buyer cares but little who produced the article, or indeed for the cost of production, provided he can sell it at an advanced price. He has his function as a distributor, which is very different from that of a producer; the two have had but little in common. Perhaps it is the fact that the merchant has usually not needed to take into account the interests of the producer that has made him so slow in recognizing the important part the producer plays in modern industrialism.

It has always been the case that the distributor received a larger reward financially for his services than the producer, but the time has come when the producer, as represented by the industrial workman, is demanding a larger share in the profits of his labor. Much advance has been made within the last few years in recognizing the justice of such a claim, and rewarding it by a corresponding compensation; but the problem will not reach its proper solution until it has been recognized that the distributor is getting a larger share than his services entitle him to. It has been contended by some successful men that the salesman was really the producer. The function of the business being to produce money, the salesman who brought in the money was therefore the real producer. Such a view of an industrial organization is apt to produce a very unbalanced distribution of reward.

The problems of producing and selling are in reality very closely linked. *If we produce an article for which there is a large demand, and sell it for a price which most people can afford to pay, the cost of selling that article in large quantities will be extremely small.* The Ford automobile is perhaps the most prominent example of this in the country. The trade papers have been full of descriptions of the manufacturing methods of the Ford shops. These methods are all very interesting and the shops are undoubtedly being well run, but probably no better run than would be the case in other factories having a similar product and output. It probably would not have been economical to develop all the methods which they have in operation without a very large output; their organization, therefore, and their shop methods are largely results of a large output, and the question which presents itself to us is—How did it become possible for them to sell such a large product? The answer is—*They sold something that people wanted at a price that many people could afford to pay.* Their unprecedented profits have proved the wisdom of this course. Just as in my former lecture I tried to refute the theory that low wages are necessary to low costs, *this example seems to refute the theory held by so many business men, that a high selling price is necessary to large profits.* The object of any business, of course, is to make as great a profit as possible, but as the total profit in the business is the profit on the

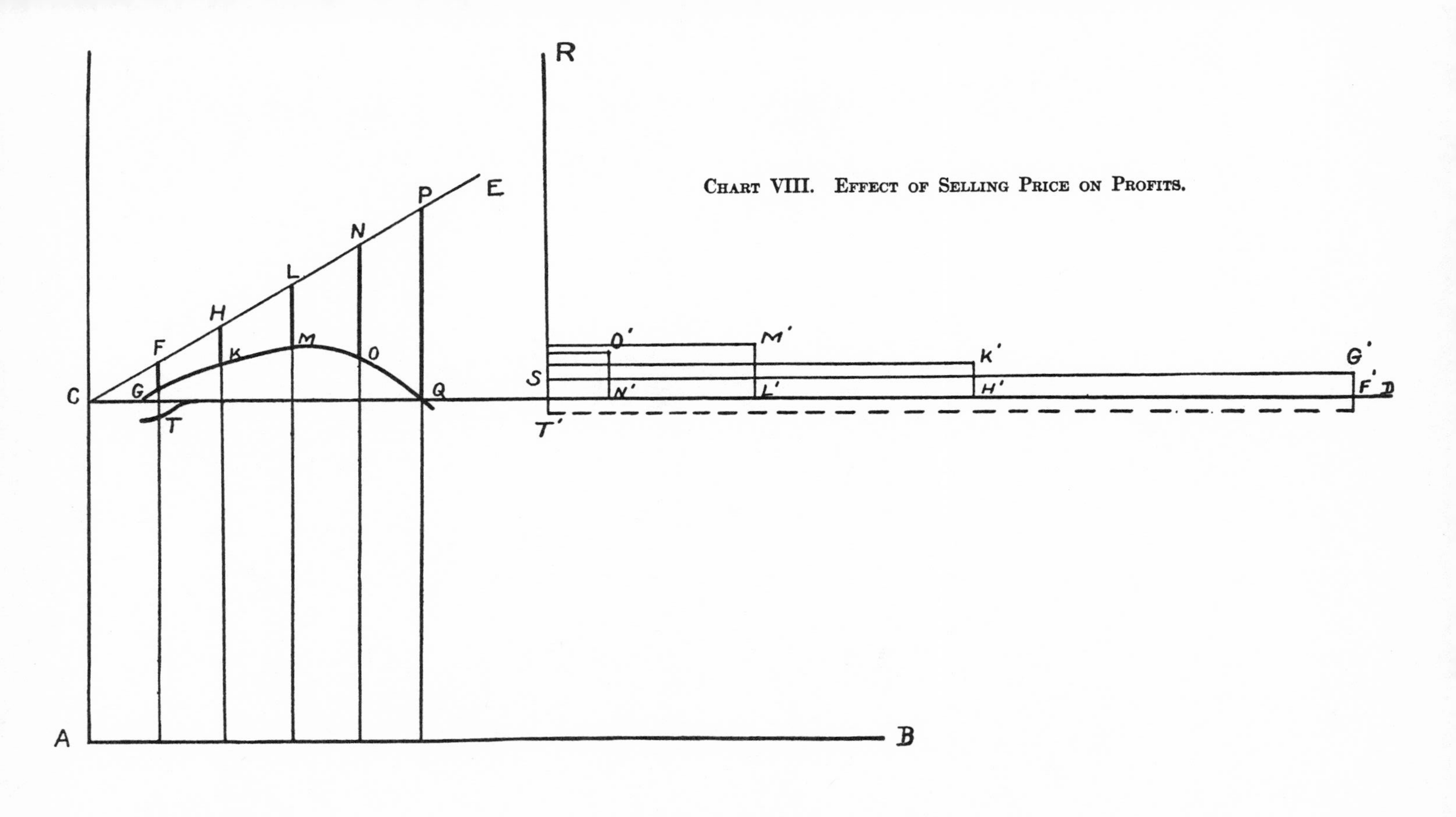

Chart VIII. Effect of Selling Price on Profits.

individual article multiplied by the number of articles sold, the real problem of the salesman is to find at what selling price this rectangle is largest.

To make this clear I have used Charts VIII and IX, which do not represent specific cases but are simply intended for illustrations.

We all recognize the fact that as the selling price becomes higher, more effort is in general needed to sell the goods, and consequently the cost of selling is increased. If in Chart VIII we represent the distance from the line A B to the line C D as the cost of an article, and the distance from the line A B to the line C E as various selling prices, we may draw from the line C E downward short lines F G, H K, L M, N O, P Q representing the cost of selling at the various prices; then the distances from the points G K M O to the line C D will be the profits realized on the various sales.

If you draw a line R S perpendicular to C D, and lay off in the direction of S D the number of articles sold at any given price, and in the direction of S R the profit on a sale, the area of rectangle constructed on such lines will represent the total profit at that selling price. You will note that at the selling price P there is no rectangle; at the selling price N the number of pieces sold is represented by S N′, and the total profit as represented by the rectangle is S O′; at the selling price L, the number of pieces sold is S L′. The larger number of items sold has reduced the cost of selling, and increased the profit per unit in spite of the lower selling price. A much larger rectangle S M′ of total profits is the result. At the selling price H the number of units sold is much greater still though the individual profit is somewhat less and we have the area of the rectangle S K′ representing the profit. At the selling price F the number of sales is still larger and the area S G′ represents the total profit.

When, however, the sales become sufficiently large, as in the case of the Ford Company, to enable us to put in special machinery to do our manufacturing, we can reduce the cost. Our profit per unit may now be represented by the line G T, and our total profit by the rectangle T′ G′. This is the kind of rectangle that best represents the business of the Ford Company. Such a rectangle can be developed in any business where there is a

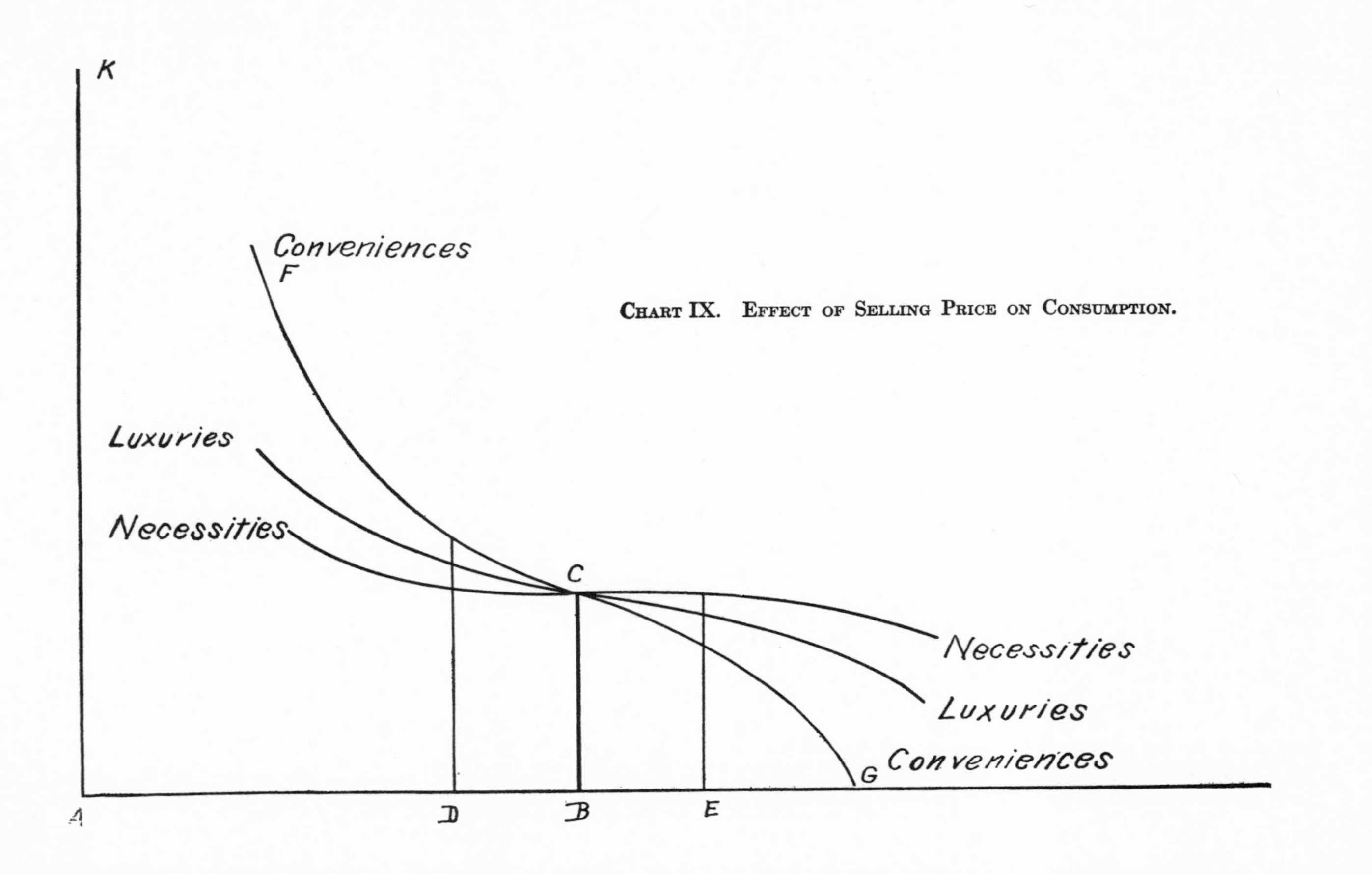

Chart IX. Effect of Selling Price on Consumption.

large demand, provided the selling price is low enough.

I once heard a salesman make, rather contemptuously, the statement, that anybody could sell a good article at a low price, but it took a real salesman to sell a poor article at a high price. Fortunately, there are not today as many salesmen of this type as there were a few years ago. The tribe is not extinct, however, and I fear far from it, for I met three of the old type together on a train only a few weeks ago. Moreover, *people are beginning to realize that there is no great ultimate profit in trying to sell a person something out of which he cannot get the value he paid for it.*

Chart VIII should be supplemented by another chart, IX, in which we represent by the distance A B, the normal selling price of an article, and by the distance B C the average number of articles sold at that price. If the selling price is decreased, say, to A D, the consumption of the article will usually increase; and if the price is increased from B to E, the number of articles sold will normally decrease. We may then draw a line through the point C in such a manner that the distance from that line to the line A B will represent the number of articles sold at the various selling prices. The shape of this line, or curve, will not only vary with almost every article and every selling policy, but will probably be affected by a number of other conditions. Nevertheless, it should be possible to get some general idea of its normal shape, and the effect produced by changing conditions. Such a curve in connection with a chart of the type of VIII for the same article should give us valuable data on which to base a policy of production and sales.

While it would be very difficult to predict the exact shape of such a curve in any individual case, the general tendency of these curves for classes of materials may be indicated.

As a rough classification, all articles that we buy and sell may be put into one of the following groups:

Necessities,
Luxuries,
Conveniences,

and the general shape of the curve for a group indicated.

In the case of necessities, a slight increase or decrease in selling price would probably not affect the amount sold very seriously, but as the price became so high as to pinch, the amount sold would begin to fall off faster. In the same manner a decrease in price would probably not largely increase the consumption of a necessity until the price was quite markedly reduced, and people began to waste it.

With regard to luxuries, change in selling price would probably have a more marked effect as to increase and decrease.

In the case of conveniences, the changes in the number used would be very markedly affected by change in price, higher prices rapidly cutting down the consumption, and lower prices rapidly increasing it.

The automobile industry is a good example of this condition, as are all labor-saving appliances. When a labor-saving appliance approximates in price the amount it will save, very few people will buy it; while if the cost of it is only a small fraction of what it will save there is a tremendous market for it; consequently, the line F G representing the sale of labor-saving appliances rapidly approaches the line A B with increase of price and has a tendency to become nearly parallel to the line A K as the price is reduced. It is unquestionably the real problem of the salesman then to find the shape of this curve for the particular product which he has to sell, and having found such a curve, the fixing of the selling price can be done in such a manner as to afford the maximum of total profit.

This problem from its broad standpoint has had but little attention in the past, for the theory that it was necessary to have a high selling price to get a large total profit has been almost universal.

If the Ford automobile had not done anything but refute this commonly accepted theory, Mr. Ford would have done a great service to the country. Whether his methods of profit sharing are ultimately going to be successful or not is an open question, for Mr. Ford's great profits have been largely due to the fact that he, like Mr. Carnegie, was the first to recognize an important principle, which was being ignored by his competitors.

Mr. Carnegie realized that if he did not run his plants at all he would lose a large sum of money each year, and that he would be far better off to lose that money running his plants than to lose it if his plants were idle. His competitors preferred to close down their plants, with the result that they not only lost the money due to their idleness, but were not ready to take advantage of new business when it came. Mr. Carnegie, on the other hand, was ready at any moment to take advantage of any business offered, and the start he thus gained made him practically the master of the steel industry in this country.

Mr. Carnegie's results would seem to throw some doubt on the soundness, from an economic standpoint, of the policy of holding up selling prices in times of depression; and make some of us wonder if it is not better in times of depression to stimulate industry by selling articles at the price they will bring, and thus shorten the period of depression. Is it not possible that the money lost during depression would be regained more promptly by this method, than by that of holding up prices to such a point that nobody could afford to buy, and thus prolonging the period of depression?

It is an undoubted fact that if a means could be found for continuing production during a time of depression, the continued increase in wealth thus produced would be beneficial to the country at large and hence indirectly to all the people. Even though the profits of such industry might not have gone so directly as before to those directing or controlling the industry, they would come in for their share on account of the more promptly returning period of prosperity. This and other questions of a similar nature are the ones which the industrial leaders of the near future will have to face, for it looks as if many of our industrial policies will shortly undergo radical changes.

Among the most serious defects in our industrial system, and one which has been responsible for more poor business policies than any other, is the lack of a satisfactory cost system.

It is a rare thing to find two concerns that have even approximately the same cost system unless their systems were both installed by the same accountant. In fact there are today almost as many cost systems and methods of distributing the "burden" as there are cost accountants, each of whom seems to have his own idea as to the function of a cost system, and to have developed his system in accordance with that idea.

There does not seem to be any universally

accepted principle on which such a system should be based. The one most commonly accepted is that the product of a factory must bear the total expense of owning and operating that factory, whether it was all utilized for producing that output or not. Some cost accountants even insist that the output of any month should bear the total expense for that month.

In the case of a plant running at its full capacity and putting out a uniform product month after month, such a system would give reliable results.

If, however, the output varied seriously, the results of this method of figuring would be very misleading, for the fixed expenses of the factory would in a lean month be distributed over a small product, and make the product show a much larger cost than would be the case when the factory was running full.

Inasmuch as production and selling policies must be based on costs, it is easily seen that under such a system both financier and salesman must necessarily be confused as to the policy to adopt.

It is not surprising then, that many managers have often gone ahead successfully regardless of the figures of their cost accountants, while others who have been guided by these figures have not been successful. It also explains the fact that some concerns that have not had cost figures, but whose managers trusted to their common sense, have been more successful than some with elaborate cost systems. From this we may conclude that unless figures convey the correct idea they may be worse than useless. This situation has been pretty generally recognized during the past few years, and numerous attempts have been made to find out where the error lies.

The result of these investigations is the conclusion that the fundamental principle on which most cost systems of the past have been based is wrong. The newer theory, and the one which is rapidly finding acceptance, is *the output of a factory should not bear the total expense of the factory, but only that portion of the expense needed to produce it.* As an illustration; if a factory is turning out only half the output of which it is capable that output should not bear the total rent, insurance, and taxes of the whole plant but of only half. This theory, which, as just said, is rapidly gaining acceptance, is most far-reaching in its effects. First among them is that the expense of maintaining a plant, or a portion of a plant, in idleness must be regarded as a business expense, and chargeable to profit and loss—not to the cost of the articles manufactured, the cost of which, under the new theory, will remain constant as long as the method of manufacture, rate of wages and price of materials do not change. Under this theory there may be a good profit on what we make, but the expense of maintaining a plant, or a portion of a plant, in idleness may be so great as to absorb all the profit and cause a loss to the business. The older system of cost keeping did not make this so clear, or the practice of buying out competitors would never have become as common as it has been; nor would manufacturers have been so ready to extend their plants until they had exhausted every possible means of getting an increased output from the plants they have. The man who can get a large product out of a small plant, is certainly in a better position to compete than he who requires a larger plant for the same output.

This fact has been so often stated and so clearly demonstrated that it is hard to understand why it is so continuously ignored. Yet financiers, who as a rule determine policies, do not seem to have grasped the idea, and are in general much more willing to spend large sums of money on plant and equipment, rather than smaller sums in putting what they have in condition to get out a larger product.

The explanation of this appears to be that the cost accountant of the past has invariably inventoried the new plant at cost, while he has not been able to place any inventory value on a system of management.

Under our newer ideas of cost keeping the new plant, unless it is actually needed to perform the service for which it was intended, would not go on the inventory at cost, but at what it could be sold for; while the expense of maintaining it in idleness would be a charge to profit and loss.

On the other hand, a system of management that enables us to double the output of a plant is of far greater value than a duplicate plant, for the double output from one plant will cost far less than if it were made in two duplicate plants.

A cost system to fulfill the needs of competitive manufacture must then not only show what we are spending to get out our product, but also *what expense we are under day by day for that portion of the plant and equipment which is idle.*

The amount of expense that most concerns are under daily on account of idle plant and equipment is so great as to be absolutely unbelievable. Such expense is truly *non-productive,* and the great need of our industries today is a system that will continually bring this *non-productive* expense, or loss, to the attention of the executive. Such a system has been devised and is in operation, with the result that the executives of the plants where it is in use, are learning things about their expenses that are most illuminating.

This system has been in operation in this country for several years in plants of Swiss origin, which are said to be very successful.

Recently I have heard that it is also in use in Russia.

In as much as both Switzerland and Russia have derived much of their industrial inspiration from Germany, the idea at once suggests itself that this principle may be in quite extensive use in Germany. Such a theory combined with their vast store of technical knowledge would go a long way to explain the success of the German industries, which their lower wage rate entirely fails to account for.

Executives have always realized that idle machinery was expensive, but in the ordinary system of cost accounting this expense has been spread on the cost of the product and was thereby at least partly obscured. When, however, it is presented day by day in a separate statement from which the expense of each idle machine may be picked out, the subject takes another form.

The first question then asked is: Is there any work we can get for these machines that will enable us to make a profit?

In case this is answered affirmatively, the problem of getting it is up to the salesmen. In case it is answered in the negative, the next question is: Had we not better sell these machines and replace them with others that we can use?

This question can usually be answered only after some investigation and frequently only after considerable time.

While it is being answered, another question arises, namely: Can we not do something on these machines that will at least partially relieve us of the expense of maintaining them in idleness? Under such conditions, if the factory manager will direct the salesmen as to the kind of work to look for, it is frequently possible to find work the doing of which will result in less loss than would be produced by idleness.

These are the problems of production and salesmanship that a proper cost system is forcing upon us, and they promise to have much influence in the near future.

It has already been said that people who have adopted the newer cost system are making the paths of their less progressive competitors hard. Certainly the nation, which as a whole conforms to the newer ideas, will be in a much better relative position than a more conservative competing nation.

There is, however, another step in cost keeping that has not yet been taken. In fact it is so difficult that, as far as I have been able to observe, nobody has done anything about it.

Mr. Carnegie is credited with the statement that if he had to lose his plants or his organization, he would much prefer to lose his plants, which could be replaced much more quickly than his organization.

Mr. Carnegie evidently considered his organization of more value than his plants, and measured their relative value by the readiness with which they could be replaced.

This is all very well for a man like Mr. Carnegie, but we want a system that will measure the value of systems of management in general, and enable us to put them in our inventory. A going plant operated under an efficient system of management is very different from a similar plant without a good managerial organization.

Our real problem is that of devising a cost system that will reduce these differences to figures. Inasmuch as these differences are fundamentally due to differences in the controlling spirit, the figures obtained will be a financial measure of the value of LEADERSHIP.

DATE DUE

JUN 14 '85			
DEC 15 2003			